NB.S.
GUIDE TO
SUCCEEDING
IN BUSINESS
—— BY ——
BREAKING
ALL THE RULES

Dan S. Kennedy
Introduction by Russell Brunson

Ep
Entrepreneur
PRESS®

Entrepreneur Press, Publisher

Cover Design: Andrew Welyczko
Production and Composition: Alan Barnett Design

Library of Congress Cataloging-in-Publication Data

Names: Kennedy, Dan S., 1954—author.
Title: No B.S. guide to succeeding in business by breaking all the rules /
    Dan S. Kennedy.
Description: Irvine : Entrepreneur Press, [2024] | Series: No B.S. series |
    Summary: "The no holds barred guide to debunking common success myths,
    developing an entrepreneurial mindset, and making more money by breaking
    all the rules"—Provided by publisher.
Identifiers: LCCN 2023035204 (print) | LCCN 2023035205 (ebook) | ISBN
    9781642011647 (paperback) | ISBN 9781613084755 (epub)
Subjects: LCSH: Success in business. | Entrepreneurship.
Classification: LCC HF5386 .K276535 2024 (print) | LCC HF5386 (ebook) |
    DDC 658.4/21—dc23/eng/20230727
LC record available at https://lccn.loc.gov/2023035204
LC ebook record available at https://lccn.loc.gov/2023035205

MYTHS & LIES

1. Think positive and life will be wonderful. Attitude is everything.
2. He's a born salesman. You either are or you aren't.
3. You can't get anywhere these days without a college education. You need the permission of others, authorization from somebody in order to succeed.
4. The meek shall inherit the earth. Modesty is a virtue.
5. Mind your manners. Behave as you are SUPPOSED TO behave "around here."
6. Be original. Be creative. Invent. Innovate.

7. If at first you don't succeed, try, try again. Winners never quit and quitters never win.
8. Practice makes perfect.
9. Luck has EVERYTHING to do with success—"they're lucky." Luck has NOTHING to do with success.
10. Haste makes waste. The tortoise beats the hare. Slow 'n steady.
11. The customer is always right.
12. You can't "get rich quick."
13. It takes money to make money.

FORGET EVERYTHING YOU'VE EVER BEEN TOLD ABOUT...

Positive Thinking

Pleasing Personality

Formal Education

Professional Credentials

Creativity

Customer Service

Quality and Excellence

Persistence

Contents

Foreword

by Russell Brunson
Founder & CEO of ClickFunnels

I t was Memorial Day weekend, and my wife and I had plans to escape to the mountains for a few days. But those plans were ruined when we walked out of our front door and I saw that our yard was completely flooded. We had a burst pipe somewhere in the ground and I had the opportunity, over the next 10 hours, to dig up the yard to find and fix it.

Now, this was years before the iPod was invented and years before we had podcasts to listen to and keep our minds entertained. The only thing I had to keep my mind off the pain was a CD player and about a dozen CDs I had recently found on eBay from a marketing genius that I kept hearing people talk about, Dan Kennedy.

I put the first CD in, pressed PLAY, and started digging.

During the previous few months, I had been trying to figure out how to start my own business. I had recently changed my major to business at the university I was attending, hoping that I'd learn the secrets of starting my own company.

Within a few weeks, a hard truth hit me. My teachers, while well-versed in theory, had never actually started or run a business themselves. They had plenty of knowledge from books, but they lacked the real-world experience to truly understand the intricate dance of entrepreneurship. It was a bit like learning swimming techniques from someone who'd never dipped their toe in water.

Moreover, the lessons they taught were from business models established decades earlier, and the market had significantly evolved since then. They taught strategies meant for giant corporations with massive budgets, not for someone like me who was looking to bootstrap a business from scratch.

And that's why I was searching—trying to figure out a different way to have success in my business. That search led me to finding Dan Kennedy and purchasing these CDs.

As I listened that day, his words had an almost hypnotic effect on me. Here was a man who had actually walked the path I was eager to tread. He wasn't speaking from theories or regurgitated textbook knowledge. He shared practical ideas and actionable strategies, things I could put to use right away. As I listened to Dan's voice, one quote in particular resonated with me:

> **"If you don't have a good model for success, just look at what everybody else is doing and do the opposite."** —Earl Nightingale

Dan went on to explain this concept, showing that the majority aren't successful, and so following their path would likely lead to the same result. It felt as though a light bulb had switched on in my head. I realized that by breaking the rules, I could shape my own narrative, my own success story.

Many people around me were starting "internet businesses."

Dan taught me that the internet isn't a business; it's a media source. I was one of the first to break the rules in my industry and start using traditional media and phone calls to outgrow every other business we were competing against.

When we launched our software company, everyone we were competing against had raised hundreds of millions of dollars of VC capital, and so we decided instead to break the rules and grow our company using direct response marketing principles that we learned from Dan.

This helped us to not only beat our competitors who had raised capital from VCs, but also left us owning 100 percent of our company, giving us the ability to control our own destiny.

I love reading stories about successful companies that grew by breaking all of the rules. One of the best examples is Nike. In his best-selling book *Shoe Dog: A Memoir by the Creator of Nike*, Phil Knight quotes General Douglas MacArthur by saying, "**You are remembered for the rules you break.**"

If you look at the core decisions that he made when growing Nike, they were almost all the exact opposite of what every other company in their industry was doing at the time.

It also reminds me of one of my favorite quotes by Rob Siltanen, which became the mantra for Apple when Steve Jobs voiced over it for an Apple commercial in the '80s:

"Here's to the crazy ones. The misfits. The rebels. The troublemakers. The round pegs in the square holes. The ones who see things differently. They're not fond of rules. And they have no respect for the status quo. You can quote them, disagree with them, glorify or vilify them. About the only thing you can't do is ignore them. Because they change things. They push the human race forward. And while some may see them as the crazy ones, we see genius. Because the people who are crazy enough to think they can change the world are the ones who do."

This book by Dan Kennedy is all about how to do that. How to change things. How to push the human race forward. How to change the world.

Not only does Dan teach you that you should be a rule-breaker, he also gives you timeless frameworks and tools to help you have success, by doing what no one else is willing to do.

Dan helped me to see business differently. He taught me to be a Renegade Millionaire by breaking the rules and the dogmas of my industry. I've watched as he's done that for thousands of other small business owners in almost every market that you can dream of. Reading this book will give you the ability to see things through a different lens. Instead of keeping the rules and hoping for a marginal 10 to 20 percent increase in your growth, apply what Dan is teaching you here and learn how to actually 10X your potential by doing things in a way that no one has tried before.

Russell Brunson
Founder & CEO of ClickFunnels

Russell Brunson is a *New York Times* best-selling author and a celebrated authority in the field of digital marketing. He is the co-founder of ClickFunnels, a revolutionary technology platform for creating sales funnels and online selling systems. www.RussellBrunson.com

Acknowledgments

The following people whose stories are included throughout this book are in my Private Client Group or are otherwise long-tenure clients. In a very real sense, they make me possible! Their contributions to this book are greatly appreciated. Their websites are listed in case you develop specific interest in any of them and wish to look them up.

Darin Garman	DarinGarman.com
Michael Huang	USKuoShu.com
Dr. Emily Letran	DrEmilyLetran.com
Lee Milteer	Milteer.com
Craig Proctor	CraigProctor.com
Preston Schmidil	GoodVibeSquad.com
Parthiv Shah	eLaunchers.com
Ron Sheetz	RonSheetz.com

My work as an author of this book, and the dozens of others with six different publishers, has been ably and diligently and patiently facilitated by my agent of decades, Jeff Herman of The Jeff Herman Literary Agency.

A FEW COMMENTS ABOUT THE ORIGINAL, FIRST EDITION OF THIS BOOK

From Rich Karlgaard, Publisher, *Forbes* Magazine:

"This book, *Succeed by Breaking All the Rules*, is terrific! Energetic, entertaining, inspiring. Best book in its genre in many a year. There are even paragraphs of your writing, Dan, that are as good as the great novelist Tom Wolfe's. And I should know. I published the original 7,000-word piece by Tom Wolfe."

From *Booklist*:

"Kennedy's campaign to debunk common success myths succeeds."

From Scott DeGarmo, former Editor in Chief, *SUCCESS* Magazine:

"Kennedy has broken the rules in terms of how much value a book can deliver—and how it can do it. Here is a book that is (1) FUN to read, (2) incredibly motivating and inspiring, and (3) quite profound. The rebels, heretics and millionaire misfits that enliven these pages guarantee that reading this book will be an entertaining and unforgettable experience. But you'll also discover how you can gain power by being different in your own way."

A FEW COMMENTS ABOUT
DAN KENNEDY, THE AUTHOR

From Brian Tracy:

"Dan Kennedy is unique, a genius in many ways. I have always admired his ability to see the vital truths in any business and to state these realities with straight-forward language and clear definitions. His approach is direct. His ideas are controversial. His ability to get results for his clients unchallenged."

From Justin Miller, CEO, Profit 911

"My business would not exist were it not for Dan Kennedy."

From Dr. Dustin Burleson, DDS, MBA

"I am forever grateful for all you have done for me, my businesses and my profession."

An Important Introduction by the author, Dan Kennedy

The Opportunity in Doing the Opposite

G ee, am I sure it's GOOD advice, telling people to break ALL the rules? On purpose? I wrote the first edition of this book back in 1997. The one you now hold in your hands or see via your Kindle® is an updated, revised, new and improved version, but the original stood the test of time pretty well. I hadn't looked at it in years, until my friends at Entrepreneur expressed interest. It sat, displayed cover out, on a shelf of antiques in my office. When I dusted it off and read it, I was impressed with myself—!!!—for having been so prescient about the future and so evergreen with my principles. Most "advice" does not age so well. I hope this rarity will motivate even keener interest in the book than if it were brand new, thought up yesterday. I included the Original Introduction here, after this one, as it had some important points I thought best expressed unchanged.

There are 13 Myths & Lies. I did not drop or change any of them. I added only one. It turns out that the B.S. that was being foisted on people about Success 26 years ago is still being promoted today. It turns out that it's hard to kill B.S. that serves B.S. promoters' agendas. That gets embedded in popular culture, in academia, and in business. Even when it is entirely discredited, it just won't go away. Kind of like the wearing of cloth masks to protect us from each other and the China Virus, more a version of putting a garden gnome in your yard for good luck than medical science. But even after being thoroughly discredited, and virtually all of its "public health expert" promoters fessing up to its meaninglessness, you still saw quite a few people masked up in public. Very similarly, the Lies & Myths and Rules about Success as an entrepreneur tackled in this book should have died a natural death by discrediting long before now. But they haven't. In fact, some of them have actually grown and strengthened and become more doggedly promoted than when I first wrote about them in 1997.

I wrote this book, and a few years later began my entire collection of NO B.S. books, out of the inspiration of irritation. It just annoyed the hell out of me seeing new authors, speakers, and experts parrot the Lies & Myths of their predecessors. Worse, these Lies & Myths lived and live as RULES. Follow the Rules, right? For me, they became the checklist of things NOT to do. In business setting after business setting, I found my greatest opportunities not only by breaking all the rules, but by doing the polar opposite of their directives. Candidly, this won't make you popular among peers. But now, after a 50-year career that has produced substantial wealth, autonomy, prominence in my audiences, and millions of dollars of fees for advising entrepreneurs—from start-ups rubbing two sticks together to those building $10 million to $100 million, even $1 billion companies—I can assure you from extensive experience: Your most likely and productive and lucrative path to success in any business will be by very intentionally rejecting and deliberately breaking ALL the Rules.

This is *hard*. We are hardwired to conform, as a survival instinct. We have been taught to conform and herded into conformance since early childhood. We have been sold, hard, on *not* rocking the boat, *not* making trouble, *not* challenging the orthodoxy. If Bezos had complied, Amazon would still just be a bookstore. If Jobs had complied, there'd have been no Apple as we know it. It would be just another IBM. From Thomas Edison to Elon Musk, the inventors of our way of life and its products and services have been rule-breakers. Still, such people are cast as outliers, not role models. So, you have had Lies & Myths converted to Rules pounded into your head, with every rebellion forcefully put down. We applaud and celebrate the rule-breakers, often AFTER they have achieved some enormous success—but we fight them tooth 'n nail while they are making their success. People who call B.S. what it is, B.S., are DESPISED by any and all Establishments that they dare question or defy. So, reading this book is easy. Living it is hard. Success of almost any kind puts you toward or at the top of a pyramid. There are 1 percent at the very top, 4 percent doing very well, 15 percent doing well enough to enjoy the game or to earn a living, and then there are 40 percent barely surviving and 40 percent utter failures. You can apply this pyramid to any population—as a financial success pyramid to, say, all dentists in America or all dentists in big cities or those in small towns, or all dentists named George. The pyramid is there. You can find it in ANY AND EVERY business, industry, or profession. You'll also find it with weekend golfers, tournament poker players, pro athletes. Everywhere. Naturally, the 80 percent diligently obeying all the rules made for them and by them despise the 20 percent who defy some of the rules and the 1 percent to 5 percent who defy ALL the rules and get extraordinary, exceptional, infinitely better results. If you listen to and conform to the 80 percent, you will be one of them. Here, I'm showing you how the top 1 percent to 5 percent think and act very, very differently, and get very, very different results.

It is important to notice this, to reinforce your commitment to breaking rules. Next time you go to Starbucks, remember that Howard Schultz broke all the rules about price in the coffee shop industry. Next time you visit Disney World or Disneyland, remember that Walt broke all the rules of the amusement park industry. Premiering in the spring of 2023, owned by "The Rock," wrestler-turned-actor Dwayne Johnson, the XFL football league broke many of the rules about how the game of football is supposed to be played. The new LIV golf blithely violated a lot of the rules of pro golf—including spectators required to be quiet. At a LIV golf tournament televised in April of 2023, a popular golfer made a truly impossible hole-in-one, and the fans went wild, even showering him in thrown glasses of beer, which he cheerfully indulged. The success or failure of the XFL and of LIV can't be known yet, as I write this. But one thing is certain: There was no room in the market for just another football league, a watered-down NFL, nor for another pro golf league, a poor cousin and inferior clone of the PGA. The only possibility of success for these "outlaw enterprises" is breaking rules, not conforming to them.

Currently, there is enormous, unprecedented pressure to conform to certain approved thinking. For refusing to do so, you can be canceled and disappeared from social media, attacked on social media by mobs, forced to comply or not be published, financially pressured and penalized, attacked if speaking publicly—say, on a college campus—even investigated by the government—the FBI sicced on parents protesting at school boards as an example. The government actually tried to create a straight-from-Orwell "Ministry of Truth." In business, there is pressure from within and outside. Activist employees can gang up on their employers. Consumer boycotts can be ginned up in social media. Despite all this, one of the most vital requirements for success for the entrepreneur is clearheaded, *independent* thinking. Success is born of objective truth and facts, not opinion or ideology. Another success requisite is focus on productivity and profit. In business success, Principles govern Strategies, then Strategies govern Tactics. You must know what your absolute Principles are, and not allow yourself to be coerced or pressured into abandoning them. This is not just about politics. It's about everything. Just as an example, if your guiding Principle is accurate measurement and accountability, by counting money, and a gang of staff or an agency or an "expert" wants you to buy a lot of unaccountable brand or image advertising or, worse, wants you to count likes or views or viral activity instead of gained customers, sales, and profits, you must stick to your Principle and call "B.S.!"

For symbolic purposes, I had aerosol cans labeled as NO B.S. SPRAY, for use any time B.S. was *smelled.* You spray it and kill it. There's, sadly, no such spray. But you need to train yourself to smell B.S.—and not let yourself be affected by it. This book will help you with that.

If you are already an entrepreneur in a business or businesses, this book can help you reassess everything you are doing with and in your company—and *why* you are doing it as you are. From that can come the realization that you are obeying some rule or conforming to some standard that is based on a lie or myth, and would be best ignored and defied. From this can come profoundly important breakthroughs!

If you happen to be an entrepreneur-virgin, this book can save you a lot of time, energy, frustration, and money from day one. You can keep your business B.S. FREE!

Important Note

I have *not* rewritten or written this book in the currently "required" style, taking care to vary the pronouns, balance the number of "hes" and "shes" in stories, replaced accurate terms like "China Virus" with deceptive, neutral terms like "the pandemic," or otherwise twisted myself up like a pretzel to try offending no one. I write like I talk. Although you can't talk back—except in your mind—I write as if you and I are having a conversation, maybe with an adult beverage, in your or my backyard. I do not write with concern over what a gender studies graduate from Columbia may think about me. IF YOU ARE EASILY OFFENDED, you might want to give up on this book right here, right now. IF YOU DEMAND SUBMISSION TO "WOKE," you MUST give up on

---

this book right now. And for the record, this means that everything in these pages is mine and mine alone. You shouldn't blame my publisher. I'm confident there are things in here that its editors cringe at. It's all OK. They and you have a perfect right to cringe or disapprove or feel "triggered," not like my book or not like me, reject it wholesale. I have a perfect right to put forward my ideas said as I want to say them, expressed honestly, authentically, and candidly. We CAN coexist peacefully on this planet. And you might apply one of my Dynamic Success Questions: "Where is the PROFIT in that?" There's no profit to be had from being indignant. There is only profit to be had in finding and using information or strategies that can advance and accelerate your success.

AUTHOR'S ORIGINAL INTRODUCTION (1997)

"Sometimes You Gotta Break the Rules"

*"Not only have I broken all the rules I learned about—
I have broken rules I didn't even know existed."*

—*Martin Scorsese*

W e are a people in search of rules. It might have stopped when Moses came down from the mountain and announced: "Good news—I got Him down to ten." But even though few people manage to live by those, everybody wants more. Even the Catholics, who have lots of rules, still want more. In Washington, D.C., it takes a building to house all the rules already passed by all of the legislators who've trekked through there, yet today a session of Congress is still evaluated based on how many more rules it gets written and passed. In the arena of self-improvement and self-help everybody creates rules. Napoleon Hill, in his classic best-seller *Think and Grow Rich*, had 13. In his contemporary best-seller *The 7 Habits of Highly Successful People*, Stephen Covey has seven. My speaking colleague Zig Ziglar has "10

Qualities of a Successful Person." In his speech on leadership, General Schwarzkopf even talks about "Rule #31" and "Rule #2."

So how good are all these rules anyway?

When You Meet the Buddha of Conventional Wisdom on the Road, Aim for Him and Push the Gas Pedal to the Floor

In the 1960s, every track and field coach taught every high jumper to run toward the bar and jump over it headfirst. Logic said this was right; obviously you want to look where you are going. And you want all the uninterrupted forward momentum you can get. But this kid, Dick Fosbury, began fooling around with a twist, a turn, and going over the high bar backwards. As he approached the bar, he planted his right foot, spun a full 180 degrees, and launched himself backwards over the bar. *Time* magazine then called it "the most preposterous high jumping technique ever devised." Of course, everybody laughed. His move was called "the Fosbury Flop." There was some question as to its legality in competition. But to every expert's chagrin, Dick not only stuck with it but won in the Olympics doing the Fosbury Flop.

> **This is not the only time that "conventional wisdom" has been embarrassed.**

The Ultimate Cliché: "Rules Are Made to Be Broken"

This is a book about cliché-busting. Yet it turns out that the ultimate cliché—rules are made to be broken—may be the most valid of all.

The story of the Fosbury Flop takes me back. As a kid, on the backyard court, I played basketball, and I threw my foul shots one-handed, like throwing a baseball. I made just about every foul shot. It took a junior high school gym teacher weeks to drill that out of me and force me to use the "correct" two-handed, body-square-to-the-backboard foul-shooting position. Doing it "correctly," I missed about two-thirds of the shots. Still do. (And he just cut the heart right out of me about that game. Were it not for him and his stupid rule, I might have gone on to play, a college scholarship, and wound up being like Dennis Rodman.)

I've always doubted all conventional wisdom. In fact, I was asked to leave catechism classes at our family's Lutheran church, never to return, because I was asking too many questions. I don't remember the guy's name, but the minister who taught those classes had really baggy pants, and I usually got him so mad with my questions he would go into a tirade, face flowing red, actually feverishly jumping up and down for several minutes. I measured my effectiveness by how far up his legs his baggy pants went.

That Kid Who Won't Stop Asking Questions Grows Up

My main business is advertising. And there are a zillion rules about how to create good advertising. There is a wealth of conventional wisdom. I have made an entire career out of violating all this wisdom, all these rules.

In the January 1993 issue of a trade magazine for the nonprofit field, *Fund Raising Management*, an article by industry expert Mal Warwick ran with this title: "The 11 Cardinal Rules of Copywriting—and How to Break Them." You do not need to read this article to get value from it. The headline alone says a lot. It reminds us that in EVERY field, there are rules for successful achievement—that are made to be broken. Let me give you a great example from the direct response advertising field. For maybe thirty years, the "rule" for a full-page, copy-intensive direct response ad was to put a coupon in the lower right-hand corner, and to make that coupon very clearly stand out, even jump out of the rest of the ad. Typically using a big, thick, dotted-line border, a bold headline like "Free Trial Coupon" or

"Order Form." Even as the toll-free 800 number and credit card ordering by phone came onto the scene, this "rule" remained and was adhered to. Until a few people, like me, Mark Haroldsen, and a couple other advertisers broke the rule. Today about a third of all such ads use the "new couponless format" we pioneered, where there is no coupon; instead, the ordering instructions are written into the copy, in a seamless flow, and the customer is asked to call an 800 number OR take a plain piece of paper and write his name, address, and other information on it and fax it in or mail it in to a provided address. But there's no coupon to fill out and tear out. In many cases, this proves to increase response—presumably because it increases readership; the absence of the coupon lets the ad look more like an article. In the late 1980s, however, I began experimenting, very successfully, with a now much copied violation of this format: couponless ordering instructions combined with a lengthier summary of the offer in a box with a border around it. This approach not only violates the rules, it defies logic. It reveals at a glance that the ad is an ad, not an article, and while it does not provide the convenience of a coupon, it boosts response. How can that be? Got me. But sometimes it pays to break the rules just to break the rules.

This Book Even Argues with Itself

Maybe the best part of this book is that it can't even agree with itself.

My friend Herb True, a management professor at Notre Dame, tells me that a lot of kids go into shock when he gives them several books to read, each one presenting a conflicting viewpoint on the same issue. They come back and want him to tell them which of the authors is "right."

On one level, I'd like things to be that simple. Just give me *one* set of instructions. On the other hand, not only am I sure that nobody has the one-size-fits-all, solves-all, handles-every-situation set of instructions. I'm also sure if somebody did have it they'd disagree with it half the time. The only folks I'd ever met who are absolutely dead-on certain that they know the right thing to do in every circumstance, for themselves and everybody else around them, are just like that Jim Jones guy who wound up leading his followers to mass suicide in Guyana. Anybody that certain of his rules is dangerous.

Still, even as we see that rules don't always work, we go looking for more rules.

Nowhere Are There More Rules Than in How-to-Succeed Land

Beginning in 1975, I officially joined the "success education industry," populated by thousands of speakers, seminar leaders, authors, gurus, psychologists, and organizations, from the very staid Dale Carnegie folks to, well, remember EST? In recent years, about a third of my life has been as a professional speaker, addressing over two hundred thousand people a year and appearing at many events with big-name "success speakers" like Zig Ziglar, Jim Rohn, and Tom Hopkins. One of my best clients, the Guthy-Renker Corporation, produces the Tony Robbins infomercials. Millions of dollars of my own how-to-succeed books, cassettes, and other products have been sold. And, in this book, I chew vigorously on that hand that has fed me and feeds me so well.

Among the classic ideas and axioms about success in business and success in life that we turn inside out and look at with a jaundiced eye here, together, many are the "treasures" of the "success industry." Some of my colleagues may very well hate this book. And that's okay with me. I figure: If you don't offend somebody at least once a day, you're not saying much. The opportunity to offend tens of thousands with a book like this was irresistible.

Oh, and about those Catholics. I was raised a Lutheran, which is a Catholic but without confession, the little glasses of wine and the cookies, or our own infomercials at Easter and Christmas. When I was a kid, we had good friends who owned a little neighborhood restaurant and take-out joint in Parma, Ohio, right smack in the middle of a Catholic parish near a very big church. This place's owners made their living off the Friday fish dinner business. From 4:00 to 7:00 p.m. an ocean of fried fish in Styrofoam containers went out their door. Enough tartar sauce in little paper cups to drown Moby Dick. We even ate fish every Friday— religiously—and we weren't Catholic. As I understood the deal, if you ate meat on Friday, you guaranteed yourself a seat in hell for all eternity, and we weren't taking any chances. I wonder what somebody thinks who hates fish but eats it every Friday, 52 Fridays a year, for say, twenty years, 1,040 Fridays, in order to stay out of hell, then gets the word: Hey, we changed the rules. It's okay now to eat anything you want on Friday. Huh? What happened here? Is hell full? Did they catch the pope wolfing down a couple Big Macs on a Friday? Did word come down from the sky: "I'm sick of eating fish every Friday!" What?

You could be following some rule just like that, which some years down the road, some authority's going to change. Just like that fish-on-Friday deal. Let's find out.

CHAPTER 1

Forget Just About Everything You Were Ever Told About Positive Thinking

"Thought is subversive and revolutionary, destructive and terrible, thought is merciless to privilege, established institutions and comfortable habit. Thought looks into the pit of hell and is not afraid. Thought is great and swift and free, the light of the world, and the chief glory of man."

—*Bertrand Russell, mathematician, philosopher, Nobel laureate*

In the 1996 Kentucky Derby, famous trainer D. Wayne Lukas sent a horse named Prince of Thieves and another horse named Grindstone to the gate, both with top jockeys: Pat Day on Prince of Thieves, Jerry Bailey on Grindstone. Prince of Thieves was picked by many to win. Grindstone was picked by no one. Prince never got in gear. Grindstone came from way behind, in a thrilling stretch drive, to "steal" the race. Grindstone, however, injured himself in his herculean effort and was promptly retired to stud, not to go on to the second race in the Triple Crown. Incredibly, Lukas then yanked Day from Prince of Thieves and replaced him with Bailey for the Preakness. This was a huge slap in the face to the all-star jockey who had won four previous Preakness races, including two for Lukas. It'd be akin to benching a quarterback like Joe Burrow or Patrick Mahomes after one disappointing game. It was the talk of the racing world. And it set up one of the great moments of sports.

Two weeks later, at Pimlico in Baltimore, Jerry Bailey rode D. Wayne Lukas's highly touted Prince of Thieves in the Preakness Stakes. As always, Lukas was much interviewed before the race, and very visible in the stands as post time approached. The deposed Pat Day picked up a mount from another trainer, and he went to the gate on Louis Quatorze, a ten-to-one long shot that had finished a dismal sixteenth in the Derby. When the gate opened, Quatorze buckled but Day steadied him, straightened him out, and took the lead—and never looked back. Day rode Louis Quatorze to a blistering 1:53½ for the one and three-sixteenths mile race, matching the record for the race set 12 years before.

As he sailed across the finish line, standing in the stirrups, he looked in the direction of Mr. Lukas, then to the TV cameras, and defiantly waved his hand, wiggling all five fingers and shouting "Five." He had won the Preakness four times. Now, five.

"Five!"

It was one of those magic moments when somebody who has been underestimated or ridiculed gets to triumph. Every Thoroughbred jockey and even every Standardbred driver in America was rooting for Pat Day and reveled in the "Up yours, Lukas!" emotion that surged through him as he pushed that second-rate horse to a record-setting Preakness victory.

Pat Day rode the race of his life, motivated not by any pure, elegant, charitable, or noble impulses. He rode the race of his life motivated by—*revenge!*

Anybody who has ever been "crapped on" can identify with Pat Day. I watched it, too. I bet on Louis Quatorze only because I wanted Day to stick it to Lukas. I was in a hotel room an hour or so after giving a speech, on the edge of my seat on a footstool in front of the TV, urging him on and yelling "Yes!" as he gave his salute to Lukas.

This same story—in different businesses, professions and sports—plays out repeatedly, actually frequently. It's why one of the most successful, most copied advertising headlines of all time, from John Caples, is:

"They All Laughed When I Sat Down at the Piano—But When I Started to Play." It appeals to the desire we all experience, at one time or another, to succeed at something in order to exact revenge against those who doubted or mocked or criticized us. **It demonstrates that a "negative" emotion can inspire "positive" actions and results.**

Most successful people choose not to talk about it, but many were and are motivated by very ignoble, "negative" emotions. I don't think any author of any of the gazillion how-to-succeed books has ever addressed this. Instead, most preach the idea that you must eradicate, suppress, or give up all such negative emotions, forgive everybody, and focus only on positive, happy thoughts. And that sounds right. But reality does not prove it to be true.

And this is just one of a number of ways that "positive thinking" is misunderstood and misused.

Incidentally, I drove professionally in harness races for 20 years. When I began, I was not yet competent, and I was unwelcome. The pros saw me as somebody dropping down out of the sky, from the clubhouse, disrespecting them by daring to think I should be on the same track as they were. "Why," I was often asked, "don't you just drive in amateur races?" Over time I earned their respect and got treated as a peer, colleague, and capable competitor. On the occasion of my 100th win in the sulky, I remember thinking about Pat Day and his "Five!" as I drove my horse, Lightning Luck, to the Winner's Circle for the photo. To him, and to myself, I said "100!" out loud. With that win, as with some others, I beat two of the leading drivers in the country.

With Apologies to Dr. Norman Vincent Peale, Here's What's Wrong with Positive Thinking

My mother was a huge fan of Norman Vincent Peale and you may be, too. I met the late Dr. Peale on two occasions, and I certainly respect his enormous influence, but I am convinced he may be one of the most misinterpreted, misunderstood authors in our genre. If he were alive, I think he'd applaud this book.

Here are the main ways people get misled with "positive thinking."

#1: "Don't Be Negative!"

This is the cry of the demented organization turning against its sole, sane voice. I have many times observed the individual who dares to raise questions about the viability of a particular idea shouted down with "Don't be negative!"

There is a joke many motivational speakers tell, as a positive illustration of positive thinking: A guy has tripped and fallen off the roof of a 30-story building. He is falling toward certain death. Someone yells out the 15th-story window, "How are you doing?" And the falling fellow hollers back, "Okay so far!" This has been told at countless sales meetings and seminars. But it is NOT an accurate representation of "positive thinking" as Peale meant it to be. It does *not* illustrate positive thinking. It illustrates *stupidity*.

The idea that raising questions, doubt, skepticism, and reasons why something may not work marks you as a "negative thinker," a cancer to be cut out, a dangerous voice to be ignored is sick and stupid.

Cynicism *is* unhealthy. Optimism *is* helpful and desirable. But blind, stubborn, unwarranted optimism is stupid.

An excellent little book by Dr. Edward Kramer, written as a rebuttal to Peale's book, is titled: *The Positive Power of Negative Thinking*. One of Kramer's premises is that if you carefully anticipate every possible way your plan or endeavor can be disrupted, derailed, or sabotaged and you proactively prohibit as many of those things as you can, and have a "Plan B" for every one you can't effectively prohibit, you then not only boost your odds of success, you liberate your mind from nagging worries and anxiety, allowing it to perform at peak capability. That last point is important. Dale Carnegie wrote a book with the compelling title:

How to Stop Worrying and Start Living. The best way I know to STOP WORRYING is to have taken time to plan for every eventuality so you know in advance what to do if any one of them actually rears its head.

If you happen to be a sales manager reading this, I have some specific, contrarian advice for you. Instead of going into the weekly meeting as a low-rent motivational blowhard, exhorting the troops to "think positive" and decrying those who dare "think negative," dig in and do a real job, so you can go in there with a marketing, prospecting, and sales plan of substance so that the troops have something worth being optimistic about.

And for salespeople, negotiators, or others who seek to persuade or influence, I teach "the positive power of negative preparation": carefully identifying and acknowledging every possible objection that may be raised, every reason for saying no or stalling possible, and every flaw or weakness in your product, service, or proposition. Get all that "negative stuff" down on paper. Then you can intelligently prepare to deal with those things. Then you will not be "thrown for a loop" when these things raise their ugly heads. Then you can reasonably and realistically expect positive outcomes.

Mike Vance, a longtime, close associate of Walt Disney, with a long, successful career as a popular lecturer on creativity, once said you could distill Dale Carnegie's advice to "smile whether you feel like it or not," but that a much better idea was "get a reason to smile so you *can* feel like it."

#2: Positive Thinking as Panacea

Having carefully read every one of Dr. Peale's books and talked with him personally at some length, I can assure you that he never meant for people to go sit in the corner, think positive thoughts, and expect riches to materialize in the backyard. Yet a lot of people sally forth believing that if they just think positive thoughts, everything in their life is supposed to change as a result. There are even a few metaphysical-leaning motivational speakers who teach such silliness. A few years back, one of these versions of the "thoughts (alone) make things" was heavily promoted and rose to mainstream popularity. Its author was on *The Oprah Winfrey Show*, her book and film heartily endorsed by Oprah. It promised what people lust for, but shouldn't: a simple solution to complex problems or opportunities. *THE* Secret. But, to be what people promoting it might accuse me of—"negative"—I promise that there is no one secret; that the only success with complex problems or opportunities comes from complex solutions. I wrote an entire book about this, *No B.S. Guide to Wealth Attraction*, with 28 Wealth Magnets. Not one. About half are about what and how you think, but the other half are about what you *do*. Some might consider this negative. I just consider it truth.

I remember getting my first brand-new car. I had owned and driven a sequence of really pitiful junkers, out of necessity. In fact, I bought my first car for $25, my second for $300. In both cases, I got my money's worth, so you can imagine what I was driving around in. Well, when I got my first brand-new car, it was a great disappointment to discover that the birds crapped on it with impunity. That seemed unfair. If I were setting up the system, I'd restrict the birds to crapping only on old, cheap, ugly cars. But birds crap democratically and indiscriminately. They're not alone in that trait.

You can think positive all you want and you are still going to spill coffee on your new tie, get a flat tire, get cut off on the freeway, lose a big sale, get cheated, and be disappointed from time to time. Positive thinking is not about eliminating all of that from life. It is a tool to be used to more effectively cope with such events, as one of an entire toolbox of tools.

People who believe you can prevent problems with positive thoughts like some magic amulet hung around the neck wind up cynical, negative thinkers. People who use positive thinking like kids use whistling in the dark to keep bogeymen away are doomed to disappointment and depression. People who insist on walking around with eyes closed to "the negative" are just as likely to walk in front of an oncoming bus as they are to fall into a bed of roses.

In 2023, Tesla recalled 1.3 million defective automobiles. Musk had that, plus he bought Twitter for at least three times its worth in an admitted bad deal, and discovered more problems with its business than he had expected. He also had the first of his heaviest-ever rockets blow up. Is it all because Elon Musk is not a positive thinker? No. If you want to accuse him of any thought sin, it'd be being too positive. But he is all about doing epic things for which a strong positive attitude is required, but without any illusions about that prohibiting misjudgments, mistakes, and calamities. Resilience is an application of positive thinking only needed in negative circumstances.

#3: Only Noble, Positive Emotions Contribute to Success

This brings us back to the Pat Day story and the many, many stories just like it of people with chips on their shoulders and somethings to prove with their success. Tom Brady, labeled the GOAT—for Greatest of All Time—never forgot he had been an overlooked sixth-round draft choice, warming the bench, possibly never getting a chance to show what he could do as a starting quarterback if Drew Bledsoe hadn't been injured. (Note: Brady had to keep himself ready for an opportunity, never sure when or how it might come.) Similarly, Steph Curry, NBA superstar, had also been "dissed" by being a late-round draft choice, and the fact that a chip stayed on his shoulder about it even made it into a Subway ad, as a joke.

The late Dean Martin, never known for his work ethic, admitted that he knuckled down and worked harder in the years immediately following his breakup with Jerry Lewis than at any time before or after that in his career, because he was angered by both critics' and friends' dire predictions of his career's demise; that everybody thought Lewis was the talent carrying Martin. Late in Dean's life, an interviewer ticked off some of his notable accomplishments, including a gold record that unseated The Beatles from the top of the charts, a diverse movie career, and a long-running television show. "Guess I showed Jerry," he said. It was a revealing comment.

I frequently meet incredibly successful people in different fields who confess, sometimes publicly but mostly privately, to being highly motivated by a desire to "show 'em."

I also know people motivated by fear and paranoia. One businessman I know, who rose up out of a very embarrassing, much publicized bankruptcy to build a $20-million-a-year company, told me he gets up every morning and works hard all day, constantly looking for developing problems to nip in the bud, and goes to bed every night worrying about what he may have missed, because he fears that it is all going to end tomorrow. "What will I do," he asked me, "if people suddenly stop answering my ads?"

Early on, I was not motivated to "get rich" or inspired by positive visions of some grand and glorious future of fame and fortune. I was, instead, motivated by my HATRED for being poor. A lot of people seem to resign themselves to being poor and get comfortable with poverty and failure. Not me. I absolutely HATED everything about it and every minute of it. I lived for a while with very "dark" thoughts about my predicament, fueling a fierce determination to escape it and rise above it somehow, no matter what it took. When I applied for my first job as a territory sales rep for a publishing company—offering a base salary, bonuses, and a company car that would make me NOT broke—I was rejected for being too young and too inexperienced by the national sales manager in town conducting interviews. I was first depressed but quickly ANGRY. "I'll be damned," I told myself, "if I'm going to let this bozo stop me from getting this." And the next morning, when he opened his hotel room door to grab the newspaper, he was quite surprised to see me sitting there, blocking his exit.

Who is to say what should motivate you? I say: *whatever works.*

There's no doubt that emotional forces like anger, resentment, desire for revenge, or fear of failure can have very unpleasant side effects, ranging from the destruction of personal relationships to ill health. But not to acknowledge that a great deal of positive accomplishment is birthed by such emotions is Pollyannaish. The real motivations behind many success stories are a far cry from happy-face, positive, noble emotions, and that's a fact.

But Here's the Biggest Flaw
of All with Positive Thinking

In 1960, a plastic surgeon turned amateur psychologist, Dr. Maxwell Maltz, wrote and had published a book that would take off, achieve blockbuster best-seller status, and revolutionize the entire field of self-improvement. His book, *Psycho-Cybernetics,* went on to reach over 30 million people, and lives on today, long after his death. These days, you can still buy the book. There is also an updated edition, *The New Psycho-Cybernetics*, that I co-authored.

Dr. Maltz came forward with the reason why so many people earnestly attempt to improve their lives with positive thinking but never get anywhere. At the time, this was a radical and controversial concept. Today, just about every book, seminar, philosophy, or approach for helping people help themselves includes Dr. Maltz's discoveries.

In brief, Dr. Maltz became convinced that no amount of conscious positive thinking or attempts at willpower and self-discipline can overcome a negative self-image. Another way to say this is that whenever resolution is incongruent with the self-image, the resolution fails. This explains sincere, earnest dieters who cannot stick to a weight loss regimen, why New Year's resolutions are never kept, why people procrastinate, and much more. It is the self-image that governs what a person "can" and "can't" do. So, for example, if deep down inside the self-image, a person sees himself as "athletically impaired," clumsy, the last kid to ever get picked to play a game, he can take golf lessons, watch golf videos, use golf gadgets, and learn the technical aspect of a good golf swing, but his actual game will "snap back" to conform to the embedded governing images of inability. Maltz was adamant that consciously set goals and consciously held positive thoughts have little power and no chance of lasting impact if they are not congruent with the images and beliefs embedded in the subconscious, and he went on to develop unique "mental training exercises" to identify what is in your self-image and to modify it as you choose. These "mental training exercises" have been used and endorsed by countless famous Olympic and pro athletes, authors, entertainment personalities, business leaders, and others. In the Vince Lombardi years, the entire Green Bay Packers team was studying Psycho-Cybernetics.

My own experience with Psycho-Cybernetics began in my teen years, where Maltz's discoveries and methods helped me conquer a severe stuttering problem where all other attempts to resolve it had failed. This stuttering kid became one of the highest paid professional business speakers in America, including, for 9 years, a spot on the #1 public seminar tour, in 25 to 27 cities a year, with audiences of 15,000 to 25,000, sharing the stage with four former U.S. presidents, many celebrities, and other top business speakers of that day, including Zig Ziglar.

While Dr. Maltz and Dr. Peale were friendly, Dr. Maltz revealed a chief flaw in "the power of positive thinking" that is vital to understand: trying to consciously force yourself to act in conflict or contradiction with the kind of person you see yourself as—i.e., your self-image—is futile.

Why "Getting Motivated" Is All Too Often an Illusion

I tell a true story about the life insurance industry. In Akron, Ohio, where I grew up, a bunch of insurance companies all had their offices lined up on Market Street, very near to a little shopping center in which there was a popular breakfast joint called The Egg Castle. Every morning, the insurance reps gathered in their morning meetings and repeated positive affirmations, sung the company songs, marched around the table, listened to motivational speeches, watched motivational videos, and got pumped up. Then, ten feet tall and bulletproof, they made a last stop at The Egg Castle for a last injection of caffeine. If you wanted to see "motivation," you had to be at The Egg Castle at 10 a.m.—but be careful not to get trampled as all the super motivated salespeople rushed out to conquer the world. If you listened, you heard things like "Today's my million-dollar day"…"I'm gonna hit it right out of the park today."

Now here's what's fascinating. In that same shopping center, there was a restaurant and tavern called The Dry Dock. There, happy hour started every day at 4 p.m. For you teetotalers, "happy hour" (sometimes called "attitude adjustment hour") involves two drinks for the price of one and free food. Any place there are two drinks for the price of one and free food, you'll find plenty of insurance salespeople. So, at 4 p.m.—whoosh!—all these reps returned to the roost. But as changed men and women. Gone was all the "motivation." Now they shuffled their feet, slumped their shoulders, looked at the ground, and said things like "Can't sell life insurance in this town. Everybody's getting laid off," "I never get the good leads," and so on.

So here's the million dollar question: Where'd all that supercharged "motivation" go?

It was an illusion in the first place.

It was what I call "motivation without foundation," which can only lead to frustration. To disappointment, disillusionment, and ultimately cynicism. While both self-motivation and motivation matter, they are fragile and temporary without a solid foundation of practical know-how and, in selling, a system for getting appointments and favorable interest from well-qualified prospects. A motivational exercise made popular for a while was "the firewalk": seminar attendees pumped up and made to feel invincible, validating that confidence by walking barefoot across hot coals and not getting burned. In reality, this is an ancient carny trick. It has no staying power. There's no real difference between it and magician David Blaine's amazing anti-gravity demonstration—it's only a momentary "effect." He can't extend it to, say, walking elevated off the ground for a mile.

This is why, incidentally, for 40 years, I refused any speaking engagement where I was prohibited from selling my "tool kits" from the platform. To get people all jazzed up about my ideas and then send them home without the tools they needed to make real changes and without securing their commitment to doing so is just one giant waste of everybody's time. By noon the next day, the floating on air has worn off. It's over. Back to earth. The invincibility is gone. Back to "reality."

The truth is that JUST "getting motivated" is futile, just as is "thinking positive."

CONTRARIAN SUCCESS STRATEGY

Give up *forced* "positive thinking" or "motivation"; instead, build a solid foundation of strong self-image, well-defined goals, practical plans, and know-how that naturally produce positive expectancy initiative and follow-through. Cultivate REASONED optimism. Have something tangible to believe in and to be excited about—not just excitement itself.

CHAPTER 2

The Myth of the Born Salesman or Born Anything

Kid to his father, about a report card filled with Fs:
"Well, Dad, what do you think the problem is:
heredity or environment?"

I s there such a thing as a born anything? Of course, there is genetic talent. There are a few prohibitions based on genetics. A giant can't be a jockey (although a 6'4", 200-pound man CAN drive in harness racing, as I did for 20 years). It is interesting how many superstar athletes there are in most pro sports who were judged too small, too big, too slow of foot—yet they proved those judgments, by professional scouts and media pundits alike, wrong.

Is there such a thing as a "born salesman"? Or someone born NEVER to be a salesman? If you look at the birth announcements in the newspaper you will see that there are lots of little baby boys and little baby girls born, but you won't find any birth announcements of little baby salesmen or saleswomen. My speaking colleague Zig Ziglar claims that when he was born in Yazoo City, Mississippi, it was written up as the birth of a salesman. I doubt it. And the truth behind the career of Zig, arguably one of the greatest and most famous salesmen of all time, is that he was a dismal failure, a complete incompetent early on.

> **Many people tremendously limit themselves and their options by stubbornly believing that successful people in different fields were "born" to do what they do, "naturals" at what they do.**

There ARE, of course, certain people the camera loves, who become successful models, actresses, or actors. On the other hand, the legendary singer Tony Bennett (whom I talk about later in this book for a different reason) is one of many entertainers who suffered from and had to overcome great stage fright. There are apparently entertainers virtually born to entertain. But even these "naturals" are deceptive in two ways: First, they are few. Rare. Aberrant. Second, even they must work very hard and do work very hard to capitalize on their innate talents.

Most successful people are definitely NOT born to do what they wind up doing so well that it looks easy and natural to others. Here are some examples:

Go back to selling for a minute and consider Joe Girard, several times recognized in *The Guinness Book of World Records* as "The World's Greatest Salesman." At age forty-nine, Joe had been the number one automobile salesman for eleven consecutive years. Here *must* be a "born salesman." But Joe was thrown out of high school, lasted only 97 days in the army, was fired from 40 different jobs, and even failed as a thief. Joe says, "People tell me that I'm a born salesman. Let me tell you that's not true. *I made me a salesman all by myself.* And if I could do it, starting from where I did, anybody can." Joe and I also share a bit of background—we both struggled with stuttering early in life. Imagine a stuttering salesman—or a stuttering public speaker!

"The Natural": As Rare as the Unicorn. As Hard to Spot as the Loch Ness Monster.

If you have been told and now believe that you have no natural talent for something you really want to do, you may be best advised to go ahead and do it anyway. After all, how do you KNOW what talent you have until you REALLY test it? Comedian Red Skelton, and singers Tony Bennett and Frank Sinatra, have all proven to be very "talented" artists. Their careers with paintbrush in hand have been every bit as distinguished and celebrated as their first careers. Fran Tarkenton made the transition from "jock" to super-entrepreneur, starting, as he put it, without an entrepreneurial bone in his body. Best-selling novelist Scott Turow began as an attorney. Debbi Fields had no known business acumen or experience when she started Mrs. Fields Cookies from scratch, yet it quickly became apparent that she had tremendous entrepreneurial "talents." I know Fran and got to spend some time with Debbi backstage at speaking engagements. I asked them both about this. They gave almost identical answers. "How can you know your abilities if you never test them?" I could fill the book with such examples.

Your past—your past beliefs about your talents and abilities, your past experiences with your talents and abilities, or lack thereof, what you've been told in the past about your talents and abilities—need only define your future if you let it. You either give or deny permission to your past to control your future.

It is best to ignore the "stay in your lane rule." My friend the late Joan Rivers had her career as a comedian crash after her disastrous late-night talk show at FOX's failure and her husband's suicide. She found her way to something that had always interested her but she had never done, jewelry design, and to the home shopping network QVC, where she could use her exceptional entertainer skills to sell her jewelry. She had never run a business. She figured it out. She had never pitched a product to an audience. She figured it out. She went on to develop a multi-product category, very big business on QVC, and also returned to stand-up comedy and to TV via "reality TV." The first success there was on Donald Trump's business and entrepreneur competition show, *Celebrity Apprentice*, which she won in 2009. Was she "born" prequalified or genetically predispositioned for any of this? Would she have discovered she could raise herself from a career and financial condition in ashes to a multimillionaire entrepreneur if she had obeyed the "stay in your lane rule"? No. And no.

I met a "natural" once. He could do just about anything on a golf course better than just about anybody else, and it came to him naturally. He never took a lesson. He could drive the ball farther and straighter than most top pros. He could putt with the best of them—as long as he was playing for fun or gambling amongst a foursome. But every time he attempted tournament play, he came apart like a cheap suit in a rainstorm. Under the pressure of playing "for real," all his natural talent disappeared. He twice qualified for the PGA, but then immediately fell apart. It drove him to drink and ruin. The movie *Tin Cup* starring Kevin Costner makes me think of him, but the movie has a happy ending. Working with this guy for about a week on a TV project cured me of any envy for people who may be "naturals." I am convinced, in fact, that skills learned and developed against initial incompetence and resistance are more reliable.

Forget All About Aptitude Tests

My aptitude tests in high school—remember those?—suggested I'd make a good social worker or a concert pianist. I happen to be devoid of any sense of rhythm or appreciation for classical music, and philosophically, politically, I'm a bit to the Right of the late Rush Limbaugh. So much for aptitude tests. In fact, the activities in which I have become very successful and from which I make large sums of money are instructive because of how ill-suited by "natural ability" I am to them. For example, for more than twenty years, I have made hundreds of thousands of dollars a year as a professional speaker. I stuttered badly for a while in my youth, I was shy (I still, frankly, am not much of a "people person"), and when I started speaking I was downright awful, awkward, and uncomfortable. My earliest audio cassettes are so bad and embarrassing I try to buy them back when I find them. I make the lion's share of my living writing—36 books have gone through bookstores; millions of dollars a year of my self-published books, manuals, courses, and newsletters are sold worldwide. And a large membership organization was built on the foundation of my writing. (Refer to the Special Offer on Page 159.)

I have been and am routinely paid six-figure project fees as an advertising copywriter. As I recall, I got a C in creative writing, a B in journalism, and my English teacher in my junior and senior years in high school suggested I'd make a great plumber. Several critics have made similar suggestions since then. And I would agree only to this extent: I doubt very seriously that I have any "natural" writing talent. But I certainly can write for dough. Instead of talent, I own what I call highly developed skills. These do not come out of the womb already installed. They are made through determination, study, and work.

I think the idea of "natural ability" is, at best, irrelevant. The argument of genetics versus education and environment is almost irrelevant. Not necessarily invalid, just irrelevant. If you are limited in a particular area, if you really do lack natural talent, you can make up for it if you determine to do so. If you happen to have some natural talent in an area in which you desire to excel, celebrate and build on the advantage gratefully. But either way, you can do pretty much whatever you set your mind to do.

On the other hand, everybody has and ought to find certain things they do better than others. Not everybody ought to be an entrepreneur, for example. Some people think they are entrepreneurs because they have proven to be unemployable. But that doesn't qualify you as an entrepreneur. A refugee maybe. But not an entrepreneur. To be a successful entrepreneur, you need to have or develop great vision, ambition, thick skin, immunity to discouragement, and the ability to live with isolation. These are not characteristics everybody would *want* to have. And just because you got cut loose from your middle management position in a corporate downsizing and you can spell "consultant" doesn't mean you ought to be one. In fact, I'm astounded at the number of people who jump into different businesses with little thought about whether or not they will like them and are eager to develop the skills and characteristics most likely to contribute to success in that endeavor. People will ask me: What are the "hot" opportunities? What's a good business to get into? But the smart question is: What's the best business for *me* to get into? Very different answers for different people.

Not because you can't. You *can* do just about anything.

Because you shouldn't. Based on who you are AND who you are eager to become. In fact, some excellent career or business advice is to pick endeavors because of the type of person the endeavors will force you to become. An early mentor used to urge people of very limited financial means to commit to the goal of becoming a millionaire, not so much for the money, he explained, but because of the people they would have to become, the positive characteristics and behaviors they would have to develop in order to achieve the financial benchmark. He was widely misunderstood on this point and perceived by some to be a preacher of greed. What he meant, simply, was: Big commitment to big goals builds big people.

Forget All About IQ Tests

For years, educators, parents, and everybody else devoutly believed in the predictive value of IQ tests. Today, psychologists agree that IQ measures only about 20 percent of the factors that determine success, so that high IQ versus low IQ cannot reliably forecast who will be successful or unsuccessful in life in general or in any given career or business field.

Eighty percent of all that determines success comes from factors that are not measured by IQ. This led to the very successful 1995 book *Emotional Intelligence*, by Daniel Goleman, Ph.D., a former Harvard lecturer and *New York Times* reporter on behavioral and brain sciences. Goleman found the traditional measurements of intelligence unsatisfactory in predicting how people live their lives. Why doesn't the smartest kid in class automatically wind up the richest? The happiest? Why are some people buoyant when awash in adversity while others crumble? With "EQ," Goleman has attempted to define a new and different standard, a more accurate measurement of a person's reactions to life situations.

This is not to discredit intelligence. However, it has been my experience that many extremely successful people are more cunning than smart, and that their developed abilities to read and to influence people are more important than their IQ. Over my years, I've met a number of Mensa members unable to get their ideas across to others, even unable to earn a decent living. I've also met quite a few high school dropouts told they were "dumb"—including by their IQ test results—who made themselves into wealthy entrepreneurs, best-selling authors, and, in one of my fields, high-paid, sought-after advertising copywriters. Tied to Goleman's "EQ," I have found that highly successful people have "made it" much more because of their mental toughness and resilience than their intelligence.

Incidentally, while it may be quite difficult to raise or improve IQ in adulthood, it is certainly possible and comparatively easy or at least formulaic to deliberately modify and alter EQ at virtually any age. Dr. Maltz's work, summarized in his book *Psycho-Cybernetics*, tells you how to do this for yourself. I have also found it enormously helpful, personally, to read biographies and autobiographies of top achievers who were not the smartest people in the room, but who were very good at getting back up after life or opponents knocked them down.

In the book *Profiles of Power and Success: Fourteen Geniuses Who Broke the Rules*, author Gene Landrum concludes that "too much money or education or IQ is actually counterproductive to achievement." How can that be? The "psycho-biographics" of the world's greatest innovators and entrepreneurs this author studied conclusively prove that intelligence is way down the list of important criteria for high achievement or attaining power in virtually any profession. A former president of Harvard is quoted as saying, "Test scores have a modest correlation with first-year grades and no correlation with what you do in the rest of your life." It appears possible to be, in street language, too smart for your own good. Such people are often excessively analytical and immobilized by all the factors that go into making decisions, unable to communicate their ideas to the masses in a manner that is easily understood and accepted, and otherwise impaired when it comes to simply getting things done.

I used to have a mentor who accused high-IQ'ers of being so smart they could spell "horse" in seven languages but so dumb they'd buy a cow to ride. It seems that "common sense," "street smarts," or "practical know-how" may overcome innate super-intelligence more often than not.

A lot of people stop themselves by disqualifying themselves, deciding that they just aren't smart enough to do a certain thing. "That," they say, "is beyond me." That may or may not be true based on your current intelligence, learned skills, knowledge base, and organized support from others. But we are not concrete blocks. We are humans, with incredible capacity to rise to occasions. Entrepreneurs have the opportunity to build needed skills or to rent them as needed, such as with temporary project teams, or to buy them, with full-time, key personnel or from vendors. You are not limited in business by what you know or can do—only by what capabilities you can organize. Nothing is really "beyond" you if you go beyond yourself as is necessary for your goals.

CONTRARIAN SUCCESS STRATEGY

Stop worrying about genetics, so-called natural talent, or what others have said or say about your IQ, your intelligence, your talent, your ability, your aptitude. You may or may not have handicaps or weaknesses, but if you do, it is your choice whether they serve as barriers that restrict you or as hurdles that challenge you to rise above them and leap over them. Not IQ, not birth order, not astrology, not others' evaluations of you—*nothing* has as much power to determine what you will do and how well you will do it as your own decisions and determination. Further, if you have definitive goals, you can find, borrow, rent, or buy needed intelligence. People with Ph.D.s in this or that are often employed as wage earners by less educated, maybe less intelligent, but richer entrepreneurs. The internet is a doorway to expertise available from freelancers. Henry Ford once said, "I don't need to know that—I have a button on my desk to push, to bring someone who does running into my office." **Finally, consider this definition of "genius" from F. Scott Fitzgerald, author of the novel The Great Gatsby:**

"Genius is the ability to put into effect what is in your mind."

There's no mention of genetic or measured IQ, no mention of raw talent, no mention of creativity. He says: SKILL. Skill can be developed. Further, he defines genius as action, not intelligence or thought.

CHAPTER 3

"You Can't Get Anywhere These Days Without a College Education"

"When I was in junior high school, the teachers voted me the student most likely to end up in the electric chair."

—*Sylvester Stallone*

C ollege graduates, on average, out-earn non-college graduates by six figures to, at most, a million dollars, lifetime. That IS an argument in favor of a college education, although a million dollars divided over 40 to 60 years of active work is not as gigantic as it sounds stated as a lump sum. Look closer and here is what you will discover: If college actually prepares you for anything, it is for a job. College does not prepare you to be entrepreneurial, and it certainly does not prepare you to get rich. There are some universities with entrepreneur courses and degrees, but most are not taught by experienced, successful entrepreneurs, so relying on academic theories and textbook case histories for your success blueprint in business is somewhat like relying on advice from poets on succeeding in the publishing business. Amongst the relatively few universities, doing a good job with this is High Point

University. Their business leaders in residence, adjunct faculty includes Marc Randolph, co-founder of Netflix; Steve Wozniak, co-founder of Apple; top executives from Domino's and Chick-fil-A; entrepreneur-CEOs of new, innovative companies like MyEyeDr.com; and, specific to the entertainment business, producers from *The Today Show* and ABC News, even actor/producer Dean Cain (Superman). HPU's president, Nido Qubein, who personally teaches the Life Skills classes, is, himself, a highly successful entrepreneur, self-made multimillionaire, and now on the boards of several brand-name corporations. This kind of legitimate entrepreneur-relevant experience at a university is rare. In the interest of full disclosure, HPU is a client of mine, its president a friend for decades. Regardless, if you or your son or daughter has entrepreneurial ambitions and also wants to go to college, please check out HPU.edu.

These days, the worth of the college degree weighed against its cost is being debated a lot more than when I was of college age. Charlie Kirk, founder of Turning Point USA, the fastest-growing organization of young conservatives with presence on hundreds of college campuses, has done a fantastic job with a very detailed, well-documented critique of today's colleges and the education they provide in his *New York Times* best-selling book *The College Scam*. No one should go into debt or otherwise pay for a college education without first reading this book.

Bottom line: A foregone conclusion that you will be automatically advantaged by having a college diploma or handicapped and hampered without your college diploma just does not hold water now. In casual conversations, when people compare, others have often been openly stunned at my lack of college degrees. "How," they ask, "can you do what you do without having gone to college?" I sometimes answer by saying I was just too dumb to know I wouldn't be able to have my career without it. Doing business as an advisor to corporate CEOs and entrepreneurs, I've been asked about where I went to college by them about 5 times in 50 years. *Nobody cared.* I was never deprived of a client or desired compensation by lacking this credential—or any other formal, official credentials. My current consulting fees are $3,800 an hour or $19,400 per day, more than almost all attorneys bill, but comparison to other professionals' fees never comes up. *Nobody cares.* The only thing that has mattered has been my ability to produce results. This matches up well with advice I got from an early mentor: "The only real financial security is your ability to produce."

I have two clients who built a billion-dollar company from scratch and quite a few topping $100 million who never attended college or who dropped out after a year, judging it irrelevant to their ambitions. And that's the key: getting "education," however you get it, that is relevant to your ambitions—and avoiding education not relevant to your ambitions.

An old friend of mine, James Tolleson, used to include in his speeches his story of graduating from high school in Boaz, Alabama, and being eager to get into the University of Alabama, where Bear Bryant coached, until he called up, asked for their course in becoming a millionaire, and discovered they didn't have one. Then he called around to a dozen other universities and, to his utter amazement, found that they didn't offer such a course either. That ended his interest in attending college.

To this day, incidentally, you can get all the way through high school and college without taking a single course in basic financial literacy, let alone how you get and stay rich as an entrepreneur. There is even a pervasive negative attitude about success ambition perversely flourishing at universities. A desire to get rich is considered crude and unenlightened by faculty, despite facts that their university is hoarding wealth in its endowment funds and that most of the facilities on campus as well as their salaries came and come from wealth.

As one of hundreds of examples, in mid-2023, an event was held at a donor-sponsored Lewiston Center at Arizona State University, titled *Health, Wealth and Happiness,* featuring Robert Kiyosaki (*Rich Dad Poor Dad*), Charlie Kirk, and Dennis Prager as speakers.

Its topics included how to get what you want via self-reliance, hard work and initiative, traditional values, civic and community service, and personal development. Although the event was well attended, a mob of students were offended by its marketing, 39 of 47 professors went public with their horror at this brought to campus, and afterward, the entire donor-funded events center was shut down and its director fired. She was told that "they wouldn't let the KKK hold a seminar—and her speakers shared THEIR values and were purveyors of Hate." If you think this opposition to ambition, self-reliance, and initiative can possibly help you succeed, then a college like this is for you!

PEOPLE WHO SEEM ILL-PREPARED AND DESTINED FOR FAILURE *OFTEN* SURPISE AND SUCCEED

The list of super-successful people who dropped out of high school or college or who never went to college is lengthy. I got to spend a little bit of time with Tom Monaghan when working on Guthy-Renker's TV infomercial for *Think and Grow Rich*, and that inspired me to thoroughly research Tom's life and experiences. I use a Tom Monaghan "marketing secret" in just about every one of my speeches and seminars. When Tom opened the little pizza joint that was the beginning of Domino's, he was 23 years old, with no college degree, virtually no business experience, no mentors, and no money. The early days were very unencouraging. First week's sales: $99. But 23 years later, the Domino's empire included over 2,500 outlets spanning all 50 states and 6 foreign countries. By 1986, it was a $2-billion-a-year enterprise. When Tom exited, he left extremely wealthy. But still without a college degree!

Tom did a brilliant thing. My friend Al Ries, co-author of the famous book on advertising *Positioning: The Battle for Your Mind*, says: If you can't be first in a category, set up a new category that you can be first in.

Tom Monaghan did that by creating a pizza DELIVERY system. Then he based his powerful Unique Selling Proposition on that: "Fresh, hot pizza delivered in 30 minutes or less, guaranteed." Pretty smart stuff for a guy with no degree. Don't you need a degree in marketing from the Harvard Business School to come up with such brilliant stuff? Apparently not. In fact, that vaunted degree might do you more harm than good. As a study in what has been done and in the prescribed way business is supposed to be done, it stands against breaking all the rules, violating industry norms, disrupting an industry with innovation.

Also in fast food, Dave Thomas, founder of Wendy's, left school after the tenth grade. He finally earned his high school equivalency diploma in 1993. But he got his practical, achievement-oriented education by beginning work at a lunch counter at age 12, a brief stint as a cook in the army, working in several restaurants, and a "break" as manager of a failing Kentucky Fried Chicken. His business grew from the first Wendy's, in 1969, to thousands of units. Dave learned everything he had to know about picking locations, hiring, managing, advertising, and finance on the run. "I know how to make a great hamburger," he said. "That's *my* experience." And he believed that marketers often "outthink" themselves. "There are a lot of guys in nice offices who get involved in complicated theories, but people want what they've always wanted. Quality. Their money's worth," Dave said. "I've kept this business as simple as possible. We give customers good food. We have clean restaurants, staffed by clean, polite people. And we offer the food at a good price. *That's* our marketing strategy."

"NO WAITING"

I have a client, investing partner, and friend who is a perfect example of self-education for success. Darin Garman has had a 30-year career at the very top of commercial real estate investing, specifically guiding hundreds and hundreds of investors from all over America to the safe, secure, attractive profits of "Heartland of America" apartment buildings and commercial properties. He has raised over $100 million in capital for these projects, personally owns tens of millions of dollars of properties, and is a sought-after expert for conferences, podcasts, and other media on his methods. He even co-founded a new bank, helped grow it from scratch, served on its board, and exited with its profitable sale after five years. In all of this, dealing with extremely sophisticated and wealthy investors as well as first-time real estate investors, Darin says he has never once been asked where he got his MBA or what university he attended. He is accepted as an obvious expert in the field, something he took pains to create from day one.

Good thing, too, because Darin's path was from prison guard to real estate millionaire, with no college at all.

In his early 20s, Darin was a guard at the Iowa Men's Reformatory, a prison in Anamosa, Iowa. Hs initial career idea was to advance in criminal justice, likely including obtaining a college degree, but after only a year seeing "the system" up close and from the inside, he was doubting that career path. With his free time, he began studying real estate by buying advertised courses on "get rich in real estate." He thought he might slowly and gradually get ready to make it a career field. But that "someday" came suddenly.

A little past his first year as a guard, he was called into the warden's office and accused of having something to do with contraband, because an empty bottle of rum had been found in the garbage can in his area. After three days of interrogation and investigation, he was cleared. At the end, he was sent into a room in the warden's office to complete paperwork that would close the file. Sitting there, waiting for the warden's secretary to arrive, he looked at the books on the bookshelves and spotted an odd title: *Think and Grow Rich*. It was an old, tattered, yellowed paperback.

He decided to "borrow" the book without permission. He took it home. Read it. Read it again. And then quit his job instantly, and embarked on his real estate business. Darin says, "I violated the conventional wisdom that you need a degree FIRST, then you can have the knowledge and credibility to move forward. That struck me as slow and I wanted fast. It turned out that the practical knowledge I gained very quickly through experience was a much faster way. No waiting."

Now Darin is getting invited to speak at colleges. At one university, during a Q&A session, a young man asked him how long he should wait after he graduated before investing in real estate. Darin asked, "Why not start right now? Why wait? The seller of a property you want could care less about your degree or how long you've waited." He also recommended reading *Think and Grow Rich*.

RESOURCE ALERT!

Darin Garman has a collection of books and other information on multi-family housing and commercial real estate investing at DarinGarman.com.

I share Darin's experience with colleges. I've only been on campuses as a speaker or as a consultant, never as a student. Dr. Herb True had me speak to his classes on advertising and marketing at Notre Dame twice. One of those times, we also went to a Notre Dame football game, then gathered afterward at his home for a reception with a number of faculty members. Curiously, none asked what college I had attended. They wanted to know how to become successful, published authors. How to get paid speaking engagements. How to "produce."

NO ONE CARED THAT HE DIDN'T ATTEND FILM SCHOOL

Every year, while growing up, he saw and made notes on over 200 movies, and by sixth grade he was writing film scripts. But his grades were terrible, school bored him to tears, so Quentin Tarantino dropped out of high school. As a teen, lying about his age, he started his career as an usher in a porno theater. "To me, it was the most ironic situation: I finally got a job at a movie theater and it's a place where I didn't want to watch the movies!" Thanks to his encyclopedic knowledge of the movies, he got a job at a large video store and quickly became its manager. While holding down that job, he got bit acting parts and wrote, sold, and lost control of a script subsequently made into a move that failed at the box office. His first big break came when an established producer raised financing for Tarantino's script for the movie *Reservoir Dogs,* thanks largely to actor Harvey Keitel's enthusiasm for the script. We all know Quentin Tarantino very well as a result of his 1994 blockbuster success, the movie *Pulp Fiction*, credited, incidentally, with the rebirth of John Travolta's career. Tarantino is a pure contrarian. He has ignored conventional industry wisdom at virtually every opportunity. His films are violent to the point of controversy, at a time when Hollywood is under political and public pressure to rein in movie screen violence. His movies are thoughtful to the point of dispensing philosophy. He has been and is a force in the movie industry. With no formal education for it.

Nothing Against College

I have nothing against college, incidentally, as long as the person going understands what it is *and what it isn't.* For some careers, such as doctors, lawyers, and schoolteachers, it's essential. They have these rules about self-taught brain surgeons. But as I said, for most it is at best preparation only to work for and thus, be dependent on someone else.

In many respects, it prepares people for an antiquated career model: getting the good job with the good company, climbing that corporate ladder, and staying there for 40 years. If you attend a university with very strong, active, loyal alumni, those contacts can be very useful to you in the future, such as in getting a job or getting hired to sell insurance. For a growing number of purposes, though, just doing what I did, what Darin Garman did, what Tom Monaghan and Dave Thomas did, what Quentin Tarantino did—just getting started doing it is the winning decision.

To avoid being caught and called a hypocrite, let me tell you that both my stepson and stepdaughter went to college. Marty is an MIT graduate and has had a very successful career in the computer software industry. Jennifer went to Arizona State, postgrad at Syracuse University, where she attended the prestigious Maxwell School of Public Policy. As I'm writing this, she's working in HRD. My middle grandson is heading to law school. None of them had entrepreneurial urges. University education was a good choice.

However, let's say that you are reading this book and you never spent time in hallowed, ivy-covered walls. **_Get over it._** That only handicaps you if you want to get hired by a college grad to be a drone in a big company, or if you want to be a brain surgeon, or, otherwise, if you let it be a personal, emotional, self-image-weakening hang-up. When I make a bank deposit, they don't deduct 10 percent because I made all that money without going to college.

You cannot possibly study the lives of the people I've just described— and the many others just like them—and still cling to "lack of formal education" as a rationale for not accomplishing whatever it is you might want to do. And, as a broader point, you must permanently stop thinking or worrying over whatever it is you lack and, instead, focus only on leveraging what you do have and on hunting down and getting whatever information you need to proceed to your goals.

Never before has self-education been as easy, and how-to information so readily accessible. The internet has placed every kind of information at your fingertips. You can even take specific college courses free of charge at KahnAcademy.org.

Take a Millionaire to Lunch

The "Apprentice Model" is still alive and well. On this, I recommend Dr. David Phelps's book *The Apprentice Model: A Young Leader's Guide to an Anti-Traditional Life*. You can get more information at: ApprenticeModelBook.com. At the very least, you can seek out the 50 smartest, most successful people in your chosen field, wherever they are in the country, and go and buy them breakfast, lunch, or dinner, beg time with them, and pick their brains. My speaking colleague Jim Rohn calls this "taking a millionaire to lunch." You can also meet these people at trade association meetings and conventions. Have carefully prepared questions based on having thoroughly researched these people. Do as Napoleon Hill did in *Think and Grow Rich*—identify the commonalities, the strategies they *all* use, the characteristics they *all* exhibit.

My friend Dan Gallapoo was a Barberton, Ohio, street cop. Now he is a widely respected, high-paid advertising copywriter and publisher of his popular newsletter, *The Doberman Dan Letter*. His fee to write one ad or sales letter is greater than was his year's salary on the police force. He got here by a yearlong apprenticeship with one of the greatest copywriters of all time, Gary Halbert. Dan served—for free—as Gary's errand boy, cat litter box cleaner, researcher, rough draft writer, and brainstorming partner. He learned copywriting, handling clients, self-promotion, and newsletter publishing by taking a millionaire to a very long lunch.

Some years ago, a young guy struggling with his carpet cleaning business latched onto me and made a first-class pest of himself, begging, cajoling, wheedling for time with me, even traveling with me to my speaking engagements. Joe Polish was annoying, but persuasive and persistent. He got a lot out of me gratis. Later, as he made his carpet cleaning company successful, then developed a spin-off business coaching other cleaning business owners, he became a client for about a decade, during which he became a multimillionaire. At one point, he had a brand-new car delivered to me as a "lifetime appreciation gift." Joe has gone on to run international mastermind and networking groups for millionaire entrepreneurs.

Some individual or some short list of individuals can serve as your "college."

Even without direct, personal contact, you can pick a few worthy models to make a deep, thorough study of. For myself and my interests in writing and publishing to be a person of influence on certain philosophies to certain audiences, I've made Hugh Hefner, Ayn Rand, Napoleon Hill, Martin Luther, and several others subjects of my thorough, serious study. I own every book written on Hefner, a bookcase full of years of Ayn Rand's newsletters, and the same for the others. As a self-promoter, I've done the same with Houdini. They have been my "professors." I guarantee that I have a better-than-a-Ph.D. education in advertising in the wall of books I have collected on the subject, from ancient masters to contemporary figures.

You can also go to work in the field you wish to exploit, in a company where you can learn a great deal by observation. Try to work in every job within the business. Consider working free if necessary. Be a sponge. Soak up everything you can. The individual who pays attention for a purpose every minute can gain 10 years of synthetic experience in ten months.

Why Getting Past the Lack-of-Education Bugaboo Is So Important

Here is an actual letter I got:

I'm twenty-three years old and frustrated as hell. I hate my job and want to own my own business. Your books really inspired me,

*but I have one major problem. I'm interested in fitness and nutri-
tion, I study it on my own, and I wish I could create products or
a business in this field but I don't have any degrees in it. I am not
certified in this area. I'm wondering whether people will take me
seriously without a degree in this field.*

This young man is imprisoned by an erroneous belief that some
authority must somehow "knight" him before he can be taken seriously
by the world at large. In the health and fitness field, we've had people like
Richard Simmons or Jake of "Body by Jake," who have reached millions
of people with their encouraging messages and practical methods—but
neither of these men have any "official" credentials behind them that I
know of. Jean Nidetch, who founded Weight Watchers, now the largest
and most respected weight loss assistance organization in America, helping nearly a million people a year, had the following qualifications: She
was a fat housewife, a formerly fat bus driver, formerly fat child, who had
tried diet after diet after diet—in her own words "made promises in the
bathtub and broke them in the kitchen." (Yes, I know you're not supposed
to say "fat" anymore. Her word for herself, not mine.) She had no "credentials" except finally discovering a regimen of eating, thought, and behavior
modification that worked. And all of the Weight Watchers group leaders
and instructors share only one credential: They've all taken weight off and
kept it off following a Weight Watchers regimen. If you line up the Top
Ten diet, health, or fitness "gurus" of this moment, with celebrity and big
income from their advice and products, YouTube channel, books, and so
on, I guarantee at least five will lack traditional, professional credentials.
They will be self-appointed experts—experts by self-education.

While the fellow who wrote to me, all tied up by his own lack of formal education inhibitions, is sitting around bemoaning his situation, the
next Jean Nidetch or Richard Simmons is emerging, creating a business
empire, and helping a huge number of people, also without the benefit
of official credentials.

AND NOW I WILL, JUST FOR A FEW MINUTES, GET "POLITICAL": THE THING ABOUT AMERICA THAT ITS ELITES & THE GLOBAL ELITES DESPISE THE MOST AND WISH TO PUT AN END TO

When you've worked with as many celebrities as I have, sometimes for days at a time, filming infomercials and other commercial videos, writing for them, and hanging out with them in greenrooms backstage at events—some dozens of times—you make *an amazing discovery*. When you spend as much time as I have with Olympic and pro athletes—champions with Super Bowl rings, gold medals, and world championship titles—you *discover an amazing thing*. And when you spend as much time as I have, up close 'n personal, with from-scratch millionaire and multimillionaire entrepreneurs, you make an *amazing discovery*. *The same* discovery. It is a discovery, *a fact* that the Elites HATE and many outright deny. Michael Moore, for example, stridently denies this fact. Even non-Elites adopting the Elite, effete, Liberal Mindset deny this. *What I've discovered is that **none** of these people are "special."*

The Elites—like John Kerry, Moore, Soros, former president Obama—believe THEY are special. Extraordinary people. Few. Rare. Uniquely qualified to Rule, with far superior intelligence and wisdom and talent *and righteous morality*. They see themselves as the "blue bloods" used to. *My discovery—which they despise—is that the LARGE NUMBER of people who get to the top in any category of enterprise or achievement are VERY, VERY, VERY ORDINARY PEOPLE* who made particular choices to set extraordinary goals, develop extraordinary skills, and achieve extraordinary things. This is especially true here in America. Other countries have their economies, governments, and social structures set up to make such success extremely difficult. Other countries have actual or in-effect caste systems. They have systems built to protect the aristocrats. The Left wants *that* for America. They do *not* want the open ladder or open pyramid we have; they want only a two-tier society: the masses as forcibly equitized serfs and the elite royalty. They believe *they* are entitled to this, and some even sincerely believe it is for the best, for the common good. A society where ordinary people—bumbling idiots who don't know which fork to use first, uneducated boobs (if not from the Ivy League), "deplorables" from flyover states—can randomly raise themselves to wealth and power seems to them like an out-of-control ship speeding through the ocean. Worse, it defies and denies their superiority. *Therefore, success stories you and I celebrate frighten and enrage Them.*

This has Them always selling victimhood, telling people what they can't do because they aren't qualified to do it, and promoting dependence, not independence. Telling *the majority of* Americans without college educations that they are incapable of top success is just one of many exercises in elitism.

Every once in a while in horse racing, a poorly bred "mutt" bought at a cheap price, usually by an amateur owner, beats a field of million-dollar birthright babies and wins the Kentucky Derby or the Hambletonian. The public loves it. The Elite "Old Boys 'n Girls Club" of Racing HATE, HATE, HATE it. *It defies and puts at risk their entire theory of life.* Well, in the Global Elites' minds, you and I are the poorly-bred mutts. When confronted about his hypocrisy of fighting climate change and carbon footprints by flying, often alone, in giant, gas-guzzling private jets, mostly to Gatherings of Elites like the World Economic Forum's picnic, John Kerry haughtily, indignantly said, "Private jet travel is *the only way PEOPLE LIKE ME* can travel. I have important things to do." Then, snidely, "I can't very well take an ocean liner around the world." With this, Kerry spoke what They all think: They are Special. The rest of us are Ordinary. Even being around the Ordinary feels to them like visiting a leper colony. When someone from the leper colony escapes and becomes a "loose cannon" multimillionaire or even billionaire, suggesting to other lepers that they might do the same, it's bad news to the Elites. Since our American System facilitates that, to their mind it must be dismantled and remade, "transformed" to put a stop to this crazy random success that stirs up the peasants.

Setting aside Their distress, let my amazing discovery motivate you. One of the speakers at my conferences, Jake Steinfeld, who rose up from being an ordinary personal fitness trainer to a "trainer to the stars," then to wealth from direct marketing of "Body by Jake," titled his book: I'VE SEEN A LOT OF FAMOUS PEOPLE NAKED, AND *THEY'VE GOT NOTHING ON YOU*! Well, I have seen a lot of famous Hollywood celebrities, athletes, coaches, authors, multimillionaire entrepreneurs, and "name" CEOs "naked," and I promise, they've got nothing on you. Often, they are quite disappointing, against an expectation that, gee, they MUST be Special. Of course there ARE a lot of barriers and obstacles to the ordinary Joe or Jane rising to top success in any given field, but in America, the barriers and obstacles are well democratized. No opportunity is restricted only to the Elites. There WAS a day here. Black entertainers had to enter through back doors and couldn't even have a room in the hotels they performed at. Sinatra stopped this in Vegas, with Sammy Davis Jr. There was a time when a college education was essential for high income. When women couldn't have certain jobs—there's a storyline in *Mad Men* about the typist from the secretarial pool clawing and fighting her way to being the only female copywriter. It's based on a true story. Most of this is gone. And even when it existed, there were ordinary people who raised themselves against it and past it. Now, so many peasants make themselves kings and queens and build their own castles, there are so many exceptions that they are the rule. But, in reaction to all this progress, we have Dark Forces; Determined Destroyers frightened and indignant about all this freedom of the masses, growing an army of useful idiots who call themselves, ironically, "progressives" mustering to put the Pandora of liberty back in its box, where it belongs. They must discredit America's Founders and its history in order to undo its damnable Constitution and Bill of Rights; they must end "free speech" and prosecute "thought crimes." However, it is still true—despite their machinations—that YOU can be as ordinary as toast but decide to be extraordinary and to do extraordinary things. Please do. Go out and accomplish something extraordinary, that commoners are not supposed to be able to do—America needs the examples.

I like to think I've done my share of this Demonstration of Truth. With only a high school education, no other formal training, no apprenticeship, I not only made myself a Success, but I did something no one else in my field and era did: I organized a "permanent" organization, association, community of like-minded entrepreneurs from which thousands of from-scratch millionaires have been birthed and incubated. In concert with that, I literally changed the way business is done in over 100 niches (shown in the book *No B.S. Guide to DIRECT Marketing for NON-Direct Marketing Businesses*). In doing so, a kid with a bad stutter made himself a top speaker. A shy introvert made himself a dynamic salesperson, speaker, and leader. I started dead broke. I've survived business failure and bankruptcy. Attacks by entrenched Establishments. I made myself into a top business author, with more than 36 books published, and no year since 1981 without my books on booksellers' shelves. Raised myself to seven-figure personal income. And wealth. I created new business models for my coined industry of "info-marketing." I've used my businesses to raise millions of dollars for charities. I have shown THE WAY to many. With no "traditional" qualifications for any of it. And that's the important part of the example. SCREW QUALIFICATIONS OR ANYTHING ELSE YOU ARE "SUPPOSED TO NEED" TO DO WHATEVER IT IS YOU DETERMINE TO DO. LIVE THE NIKE SLOGAN. *JUST DO IT.*

CONTRARIAN SUCCESS STRATEGY

If you have a good education, by all means make the most of it. But never use lack of formal education as an excuse, and never let yourself feel inferior to those with better, formal educations. There is abundant proof that you can reach just about any heights in business without college or even a high school education if you will do the things necessary to otherwise obtain the information and master the skills specifically relevant to your objectives.

CHAPTER 4

Modesty and Humility May Be Admirable Qualities in a Monk, but Not in an Entrepreneur

"The meek shall inherit the earth…but not in our lifetimes."

—Mike Todd, Hollywood impresario

"Timid salesmen have skinny kids."

—Zig Ziglar

Maybe you were raised in a family environment where modesty and humility were taught and valued as virtues. Maybe you were conditioned early on with "speak only when spoken to," "bragging is a sin," "don't blow your own horn," "modesty is a virtue," and so on. I find that this conditioning is inhibiting, even crippling for many people when they enter the competitive, entrepreneurial environment.

When you set out to do something of significance, you will most often meet with massive resistance right from the get-go. Naysayers, doubting Thomases, and critics inside the four walls of your own home, at work, from bankers, vendors, whoever. You will likely be challenged every step of the way. Then, if you get past that, you will find vying for attention in a cluttered marketplace full of jaded, sated consumers tough sledding for the modest and humble. Overcoming all this requires a certain amount of arrogance, believing that you are right even when the world says you are wrong and that you have something important to say even if you are initially greeted with indifference.

Arrogance Is an Almost Essential Success Characteristic

P. T. Barnum said that nothing much gets accomplished without "bally-hoo," his word for loud and aggressive promotion or self-promotion. Of his time, Thomas Edison became known to the public as the world's greatest inventor, not by staying locked in a laboratory inventing, although he was persistent at that, but by an enormous amount of self-promotion and staged and hyped "reveal events" for each new invention. More recently, Steve Jobs and Elon Musk have borrowed liberally from the Edison playbook. You don't just know their work or their products. You know *them*. You don't know them by accident. You know them because they purposefully set out to make you know them. In finance, Warren Buffett has also used Thomas Edison's playbook to become widely known as "the world's greatest investor."

Countless skilled magicians have labored in oblivion while Houdini made himself "the world's greatest magician," and, today, David Blaine has followed Houdini's playbook. Inside the magic industry, countless envious, even bitter, unknown, low-paid magicians will tell you that Houdini wasn't even a very skilled magician at all and will grouse that Blaine is a much better promoter than magician. You can get the same reaction in a room of psychologists by bringing up Dr. Phil; a room of personal growth authors and speakers by bringing up Tony Robbins; for years, a room of comedians by bringing up Jay Leno. What gripes all the peers who labor in oblivion the most is what they see as the sheer, unjustified arrogance of these people, daring to put themselves out there as "the best," deserving of celebrity, prominence, and fortune when they are, in truth, "inferior."

This reflects a fundamental misunderstanding of how the world works and how success is really made, a misunderstanding I'm trying to correct in this chapter and with this entire book.

When I was on the #1 seminar tour in America, one of the two permanent speakers appearing in every city, to combined audiences of over 500,000 people a year, quite a number of my peers complained amongst themselves behind my back, some to my face, about me being there in place of many "much better" speakers and much better qualified experts—including them. And worse, me having the unmitigated gall to present myself as THE most important speaker of the entire day and THE leading expert in my field. I freely admit, there were "better" speakers. That was not the key to being on the tour. I had that coveted opportunity and owned it for nine consecutive years for two reasons having nothing to do with my comparative speaking skill or talent. Those details are too micro-specific to matter to you, but knowing the reason I wasn't there does.

I'll make a similar admission about the book you are reading right now, the entire NO B.S. book series, and my 40+ years as an author in print: There are undoubtedly "better" writers. There may be smarter business advisors. There are huge numbers of consultants, business coaches, and other experts laboring in oblivion. Trying, but never even getting a publisher—I've had 5 book publishers. 36 books published. Why? Because I have, through self-promotion, built a loyal, interested following that can be counted on to buy books, so publishers can, with great confidence, forecast the minimum possible number of copies that will be sold. Also, I'm good at Barnum's ballyhoo, and actively promote each book. In short, I'm investable. And this is all based on me being, if you like, ARROGANT enough to believe I have important enough, valuable enough, different enough things to say that I should have yet another of my books published while so many others get their manuscripts returned with rejection slips. I'm arrogant enough to believe that, as the lion says in *The Lion King*, I'm surrounded by idiots, and that I should be paid heed to above all others. If you will really understand why this book is in your hands or on your Kindle, that'll be more valuable to you than the contents of all its pages!

Why and How <u>Not</u> to Be Meek or Modest

I hope you've watched the streaming series *The Marvelous Mrs. Maisel*. It is loosely based on or at least inspired by my friend Joan Rivers. Joan made herself the most famous female comedian and one of the most famous comedians of any gender at a time when women were third-class citizens in comedy, not considered worthy of main stages, and pushed to bad venues for little money or into the writers rooms to labor in oblivion making men funny. For quite a while, pretty much everywhere Joan went, she wasn't welcome. There was a prevailing idea in the industry that "people didn't want to see *women* doing comedy." While many other women meekly accepted this, Joan did not. Her motto was: If there's no door open to walk through, make one.

In many ways, a client of mine, Dr. Emily Letran, reminds me of Joan. Not that she's funny, but that she is anything but meek and has had to overcome a lot of prejudices and obstacles to achieve her incredible success. I would describe her as unassuming, but she is surprisingly fierce.

She was born in 1968, in war-torn Vietnam. Her pregnant mother was running for a bomb shelter during the Tet Offensive. Emily escaped the Communist regime at age 13, by boat, landing in Malaysia after a week at sea, surviving on rationed sips of water. After months in a refugee camp, she made it to America. She started in 8th grade speaking minimal English, but by 12th grade she was in Honors English and graduated valedictorian. It's important to remember that the American people had, at best, mixed reactions to Vietnamese immigrants at that time.

She decided to become a dentist, at a time when women dentists were not common. And the idea of a Vietnamese female dentist was pretty outrageous. She finished undergrad in three years, and then finished DDS and MS, Oral Biology, in the same four years, in 1993. Just four years later, she bought her first dental practice—at a time when women practice owners were not common. Standing firm and pushing back against resistance marked her years in school and in dental jobs immediately afterward.

Since then, she has come to be a very entrepreneurial dentist, buying, building, and selling practices and their real estate, and making herself a multimillionaire in the process. She has also raised a family she's proud of, and in 2023, bought a practice to partner with her daughter, who had just graduated from college.

Dr. Letran has often been underestimated, told "no," and criticized for "trying to have it all" and judged because she wants things her way. She is petite, as I said, Vietnamese, and a woman. In her second business and career, as a practice consultant, business advisor, and personal performance coach to dentists, she is often, initially, not taken seriously. She is also controversial. One of her books and courses is titled *The Modern Woman: To Have It All with No Sacrifice* and advocates an untraditional, guilt-free "blueprint" for the entrepreneurial woman confronting the competing priorities of career success ambition, marriage, raising children, managing the home, and managing social life, and the critical judgment that comes from many quarters about her handling of it all.

Her life has been full of chances taken, biases overcome, and outsized success achieved. Her book *From Refugee to Renaissance Woman* tells her inspiring story in detail.

Today, she specializes in coaching other entrepreneurial dentists with multi-office practices and, separately, sometimes overlapping, women dentists who own their own practices. She is known as a tough coach, intolerant of excuses, a product of experience begun as a penniless refugee to CEO of a multi-office, multimillion-dollar business and an author, lecturer, and consultant. She is blunt, straightforward, and demanding and produces dramatic results.

In both businesses—her dental practices and her coaching—she has immodestly, aggressively promoted herself, securing features in magazines from *Top Doctor* to *Dentistry Today* to *Forbes*. Won numerous awards including Asian Women Entrepreneur of the Year. Authored books for consumers and dental patients and others for professional peers. Lectured at state dental association and entrepreneur conferences. It is fair to say that her prominence, success, and wealth are all products of her relentless, extensive ballyhoo!

RESOURCE ALERT!

Dentists can obtain information about practice growth and business acceleration strategies at TodayInfluencer.com. Others interested in Dr. Letran can find her books and free resources at DrEmilyLetran.com. A free High Performance Assessment is available at BestYouBestBusiness.com.

How to Respond to Skepticism

Many times during your career and life, you will be met with skepticism. Someone will try to back you down. Every successful person reported on in this book has had many opportunities to meekly accept others' skepticism about them.

I had one of these experiences a number of years ago, when I was negotiating the takeover of a very troubled company, sitting in the office of the president of the bank, discussing assuming liability for the company's millions of dollars of debt. At the time, I did not possess a million dollars or anything close to it. I was also young and relatively inexperienced. He looked at me and said: "I don't see anything in your resume that qualifies you to run this company. What makes you think you are smart enough to turn it around?" I answered: "I would have been smart enough not to let them get into me for a million dollars in the first place." I quickly described both the bank's and the big-8 auditors' failure to understand the business, causing them to accept assets on the balance sheet that were actually worthless. The situation was much worse than the bank executive in charge of this account knew. I didn't make a friend, but I closed the deal. That's the kind of arrogance I'm talking about.

If you are not prepared to look anybody and everybody in the eye without blinking and tell them that you are the best at what you do and that you know your stuff, somebody's going to kick your butt and send you home early. And if you are not going to knock down doors, holler at the top of your lungs, make a miserable pest out of yourself, and do whatever else is necessary to attract attention and get your message across, the marketplace will simply pass you by.

Selling YOU, INC.

Whatever you think of them, you have to understand that Donald Trump became the most unlikely and improbable president of the U.S., Elon Musk became widely thought of (as I write this) as the smartest genius of geniuses, and other contemporary leaders of fields came to hold those crowns all by arrogant self-aggrandizement and self-promotion. Some would say "obnoxious" in place of arrogant, and eye 'n ear of beholder prevails, yet you cannot ignore extraordinary results and causes to consequences.

You may not *like* this. I didn't, once upon a time. One of the all-time top, highest-paid, and most gossiped and speculated about freelance copywriters, a peer, Gary Halbert, enunciated it very clearly to me this way: "The poorly paid and average paid people in our field are all in the copywriting business. I'm not and you aren't. I'm in the Gary Halbert business and you are in the Dan Kennedy business, and we have, as our deliverable, copywriting work. But we are in the self-aggrandizement and self-promotion business. Never forget it."

This is a lot more than a semantics exercise. This is of major importance—how you come to understand the business you are *really* in, and the business that almost all top 1 percent and top 5 percent earners are in, is the very first hurdle of understanding the race.

This also links to another, very big problem for a lot of business owners, entrepreneurs, salespeople, consultants, doctors, other professionals, and service providers. They are timid, meek, and reluctant to charge what their time and expertise is worth. They have guilt and insecurity about their fees or prices, and anxiety about asking, no, expecting and demanding, to be paid.

The Number One Hang-Up

Over the years, I have watched countless different kinds of businesspeople underprice their products and services or procrastinate endlessly over making obviously, painfully necessary price increases. I have seen artists, writers, craftspeople, consultants, doctors, every imaginable expert 100 percent confident of his expertise but 100 percent chicken when it comes to setting prices and asking customers, clients, or patients to pay those prices. I think more people have more hang-ups about asking for money than about any other subject.

Some years ago, I advised a client providing a particular specialized service to raise his fee from the $500 a day he was getting to $2,500 a day in one leap. Against the will of every fiber in his being, and in dry-mouth fear, he did just that, and announced his new fee to his clients and his marketplace. He lost only a few clients but gained better replacements, and heard grumbling from only a few more; most continued to hire him without complaint; a few asked why he had waited so long to start charging what his service was obviously worth! This is far from an isolated, odd incident. I often find that price restructuring to 3X, 5X, even 10X is possible. His—and others'—price resistance was in their imaginations!

In my book *No B.S. Wealth Attraction for Entrepreneurs*, I write a lot about breaking the Work-Money Link. Business owners are indoctrinated in thinking about fees or prices and hours of work as tightly linked, but in most cases, the customer's value is not affected by the amount of time it takes for the completed service, but in the significance of the results. If fixing my golf swing so I can hit the ball farther and straighter than ever before is important to me, and you can accomplish that as an instructor, is the value more if it takes you ten hours of lessons than if you can do it in two? No. And THAT is what you have to get out of your own head. I wrote an entire book about this, too: *No B.S. Price Strategy*.

In my own professional practice, I do sell the consulting at an hourly and daily rate—as I write this, $3,800 an hour or $19,400 per day—but I price the copywriting work often created by the consulting by the project, not by the hour. If a project's fee is $100,000, that has to reflect the client's use of that work being worth a multiple of the fee to him. If it takes me one or two hours or ten days, that is irrelevant to him. In fact, it's none of his business.

This is all very important because, when you change your math, you can change your life. You only have so much time to sell and to use to deliver whatever expertise or services or products you sell. You only have a finite amount of time to manage your company and staff. That is a limit set in stone. It is what amount of income you can convert that time to where all the elasticity lies. One client of mine's company has installed its product 80,000 times. A $12 difference down or up in the price equals one million dollars down or up. If +$12, and all that money banked, it makes the owner a net cash millionaire. There are other paths to the same effect. If you live in a state with no income tax, instead of one with a high state income tax, you may be talking about a millionaire difference over your working years. I have a client, Paul Gough, now helping physical therapy practice owners opt out of insurance and operate cash practices, thereby stopping insurers from dictating their fees and forcibly discounting the reimbursements. This decision, while a bit daring and controversial, has given hundreds of PTs a much higher income from fewer patients, less overhead, and zero hassles with insurers. There are *a lot of* ways that changing your math can change your life!

> In business, you must do everything you can to protect your ideas, information, and interests and to obtain full, maximum compensation for your knowledge and expertise. The respect granted you is the respect you command and demand.

Of course, you want to go the extra mile in delivering greater service than your customers could possibly have expected. Of course, you want to provide your employees with every possible opportunity to excel, advance, and feel rewarded. That is simply prudent investment. It's the ante to be in the game. Nothing says, however, that deliberately, accidentally, or fearfully charging less than the buyer's value received will be of any benefit.

Don't Undervalue What Is "Common Knowledge" to You but Very Uncommon Knowledge to the Other Guy

Mark McCormack created the International Management Group with $1,000 and a handshake, then guided it to becoming a multimillion-dollar, global corporation leading in the professional representation and management of athletes and entertainers as well as commercially sponsored, made-for-TV sports events. It was the first such business done in a big way rather than one-man shops. *Sports Illustrated* called Mark "the most powerful man in sports." I appeared as a speaker on several programs with Mark McCormack, and I was always impressed with the down-to-earth practicality of his advice. Today, were he here, he'd marvel at what his "invention" has turned into: a huge industry dealing with tens of billions of dollars a year. Individual athletes and entertainers are industries unto themselves. The limits of what an athlete or entertainer can charge for his services, for performing, for licensing his name, for appearing in commercials keep proving endlessly elastic.

This fact of price/fee elasticity can be found in nearly every business or profession, but particularly those where knowledge is being rented or purchased.

In his book *What They Don't Teach You at Harvard Business School,* Mark wrote about his own learning curve on this issue:

> *"Many companies fail to place a premium on the real dollar worth of their expertise, or what it would cost an outsider to learn what they already know. So did we for about ten years. During that time, we had been involved with more than a thousand companies in one sports promotion or another. We had amassed an enormous body of knowledge as to how companies should go about realizing their marketing goals through sports. And we often gave away this knowledge. If a company signed on John Newcombe, for example, and then didn't know how to use him, for everyone's sake we had to step in and show them.*
>
> *"By the early 1970s we recognized that more and more companies wanted to get into sports but had no idea how to do it.... We finally began charging for our expertise. Today, our consulting division is our fastest growing company.... If companies took the time to realize the true worth of their expertise, they could use it for growth opportunities which might otherwise be overlooked: as a separate profit center, such as we made of our consulting division; as an add-on to goods or services; as a sales incentive."*

But you cannot use it for any of those things if you give it away.

One of my favorite metaphysical authors, Stuart Wilde, says, "If they show up, bill 'em." It is my experience that people do not—and maybe they cannot—place value on or extract value from advice, ideas, information, or services given to them free of charge. The less of that you do, the better for everybody.

How Much *Are* You Worth?

We are conditioned to think in terms of X dollars per hour.

This is undoubtedly how you were paid in your first job or first few jobs. It may still be the way you are paid now. Or, even if you are a salaried employee, I'll bet that occasionally you mentally convert your paycheck into dollars per hour as sort of a checkup on how well you are doing. This is deeply ingrained in many people. It is also very limiting.

How much is Dr. Letran's years of successful evaluating, buying, growing, selling practices, negotiating leases or purchases, acquiring the real estate, building top-performing staffs, acting as CEO of a multi-office company, and converting it all to personal wealth worth to a dentist just embarking on such a journey, just readying to buy or open a second office? How much, if she were alive, would getting Joan Rivers' best advice on a career in comedy, having her critique and help rewriting your routine, and make a few phone calls on your behalf be worth? Does the time involved matter?

Mark McCormack tells the story of Picasso, asked in a restaurant to scribble something on a napkin; the woman offered to pay whatever it was worth. He scribbled and asked for "$10,000."

"But it only took thirty seconds," she protested.

"No," Picasso replied. "Forty years and thirty seconds."

I had a similar experience once in my ad copywriting career. I agreed on a waived fee and a royalty on sales increase for fixing and improving a CEO's main, complex direct-mail piece. At the same lunch, I made one change to the outside of the envelope. I was later paid tens of thousands of dollars. What I knew to do was a lot more valuable than what I did.

You may be like many people—you may feel you do not have any expertise that is worth any serious money. Odds are, you're wrong. When I teach people how to become consultants, I point out that there are over 2,000 different consulting specialties and that just about everybody has some kind of education, experience, or expertise that can provide the basis for a consulting practice. Just as an example, I know a woman who stayed at home and raised four kids, including a pair of twins, then wanted to go back out into the workplace. She was such an efficient, highly organized person—out of necessity, obviously—she began consulting, going into homes and sometimes offices and helping people get organized, at $150 an hour. With no resume and a high school education, in the regular job market she'd have been lucky to get an entry-level job with about $150 a week in take-home pay. But by recognizing the real value of her expertise, she's been able to earn that much per hour. Later, she created a business training and "certifying" other professional organizing consultants, completely separating her conversion of knowledge to income from time. It made her a millionaire several times over in 24 months.

But what if you are not a consultant like me—or her—and don't want to be? What if you are a clothing salesman in a menswear store? If you are smart, you will maximize your value by becoming truly, genuinely expert in assisting men at looking their very best, by choosing the right colors, patterns, and fabrics for the right person, by being able to perfectly coordinate suits, shirts, ties, and shoes, and by being the most knowledgeable individual around on fashion trends. All of that is certainly worth 100 or 200 dollars an hour. No, you may not be able to directly charge for it.

But, as Mark McCormack points out, you can use it as added value, as an incentive for clients to do business with you and return to you every single time they are ready to purchase clothing. You can write a book, *Great Tips to Look Your Best, for Influence and Power*, you can put out a monthly newsletter for your customers and local media, you can position yourself as a "Professional Image Consultant," you can lecture to local groups, get on talk shows, and you WILL be perceived differently by your customers. You can begin training your customers to call you for an appointment rather than just dropping in. You can gain such control over your loyal clientele that you become a "franchise player" to your employer, so you can work four-day weeks instead of five and make just as much money. You can sell or value-add a complete wardrobe analysis and consultation, via home visits. And you will change your life. If you are going to achieve exceptional success, especially exceptional financial success, you have to break completely free of wage-earner thinking.

CONTRARIAN SUCCESS STRATEGY

Give to charity, but never give in business. Place the highest possible value on your expertise and confidently present that value to the world. When they show up, charge 'em. The meek and the humble may be very talented and capable but will all too often be overlooked or undervalued. Arrogance and self-promotion are necessary to advance in just about any business environment.

CHAPTER 5

"Mind Your Manners" and "Behave"—or Is Being Aggressive, Rough Around the Edges, and Disruptive One of the Great Unsung Secrets of Success?

"Until you take control of your own life, someone else will."

—Jack Welch, Industrialist

Because I routinely recommend it as "must reading," a lot of people have told me over the years that they have never read Robert Ringer's book, *Winning Through Intimidation*, because they are offended or turned off by the title, by the very idea of intimidation. Maybe for this reason—although I hope not—Ringer changed the title. The current edition is *To Be or Not to Be Intimidated?* I often refer to it as THE question of life.

I suppose we have all been raised with the "politeness ethic." I know that I was. And I have often been chided and cautioned about being too aggressive, abrasive, arrogant. Warned about losing my temper. Urged to avoid offending others at any cost. I am now 69 years old. I've had a 50+-year career. From that, I can assure you that this is terrible advice.

Is He an Egotistical Blowhard in Buckskin or America's Greatest Contemporary Trial Lawyer with Rare Insights into the Human Condition?

I have met and had opportunities to chat privately with Gerry Spence, as we have appeared as speakers at a number of events. Spence is the buckskin-jacketed defense lawyer with the "aw, shucks" country boy persona whose fame multiplied during the O. J. trial, as Spence appeared regularly on cable TV commenting on the matter.

Randy Weaver. Ruby Ridge. Cause celebre for the militia movements. On April 13, 1994, Randy Weaver walked into a Boise, Idaho, courtroom facing charges of murdering a U.S. marshal during the siege, owning and selling illegal weapons, conspiracy, and a few other crimes, and he was already convicted in the media and in the public eye, with his actual courtroom convictions viewed as little more than a tiresome little formality to be taken care of. But for 42 days, Gerry Spence defended Randy Weaver. Prosecuted the FBI and the federal government. Mesmerized the jury with the kind of courtroom tactics and dramatics more typical of old *Perry Mason* black-and-white TV show reruns than real life. The jury acquitted Weaver of all charges. Gerry Spence also won a $3.1 million damage award for Weaver from the federal government. It was a typical Spence case: the misunderstood, oppressed, victimized "little guy" against big government run amok or a big, callous corporation. It's a role he is familiar with, comfortable with, and passionate about. And he has yet to lose any such high-profile cases.

My own experiences with Gerry Spence, limited though they may be, have been fascinating to me. When he came into "the greenroom," the speakers' waiting room backstage at a seminar, his presence took over the room. He is larger than life. In keeping with every criticism I've ever read of him, his ego seemed larger than life, too. Backstage he is attention commanding and attention greedy. Onstage, while holding an audience of 15,000 in his hand, and coming across as most humble, there is still also arrogance—the first time we were on a program together, he deliberately ignored the meeting planner's instructions and the huge blinking digital timer and went a whopping 20 minutes over his allotted time. The second time, given stern instructions, the flashing timer, and a staff person pacing in front of the stage at his cutoff time, he did wind up, but he let the audience know he was being "forced" to cut his remarks short and that he wasn't pleased about it. Yet, he has personally been very courteous and gracious to me. And I must tell you: He delivers the goods. His speech was excellent and meaningful. His book *How to Argue and Win Every Time* is so good, I bought copies for my clients. If I were in big legal trouble, I'd want Gerry Spence, insufferable ego be damned.

Things like this cause many to view him as arrogant: Showing off his huge, *Architectural Digest*–featured home, he told a *Playboy* interviewer, "You see this house and whatever else I have. It all comes from insurance companies. That's like an Indian hangin' out his scalps. These are my f-ing scalps."

Spence is gentle when playing to an audience in person, to 12 or 12,000, or on TV. But in individual relationships, in conducting business behind the scenes, he is anything but gentle. I cannot imagine anybody intimidating Gerry Spence. I can imagine Spence intimidating a lot of people.

Upsetting Applecarts

You have heard that advice: Don't upset the applecart.

Jerry Jones came from Texas's rival state, Oklahoma, bought the Dallas Cowboys, and promptly, clumsily, gracelessly fired the legendary Tom Landry, immediately raising the ire of season ticket holders, fans, players, the media, and a few million other Texans. He hired an untested college coach with an ego nearly as big as his own—changing the explanation about the hole in the roof of Texas Stadium from the familiar "so God can look down and watch his favorite team play" to "so the sides can stretch and expand to accommodate Jones's and Johnson's egos." This further angered Texas. His peer owners and the management of the NFL were not at all pleased with Jones's brash disregard for the way business was supposed to be done. He was upsetting applecarts left and right.

Jones said, "This isn't a law firm or a medical practice. It's a football team. And in order to take it out of its nosedive and bring it back up again I had to find the best qualified management available. And that was me."

After the Jones-Johnson leadership took the Cowboys to winning two Super Bowls and returned the Cowboys to glory and won forgiveness for Jones, he, in a fit of ego, canned Johnson and replaced him with another college coach, this one also egotistical and bombastic, but also highly controversial, and also from Oklahoma—again enraging the fans and stunning the media. You just do *not* fire a head coach who has just won two Super Bowls.

Jerry Jones has also managed to piss off most of the other NFL owners he shares the cash cow we call "pro football" with, challenging one of the key, cornerstone tenets of the league, revenue sharing, and going outside of the league to cut incredibly lucrative sponsorship deals with major corporations. Jones suggests that other owners are lazy and incompetent when it comes to marketing their teams. In a number of ways since, Jones has openly defied the written and just understood rules.

How NOT to Win Friends in "the Establishment" of an Industry

I have a longtime client who, in the real estate industry, has behaved a lot like Jerry Jones.

Craig is a college dropout who experimented with various occupations unsuccessfully before finally deciding to follow his father's footsteps into real estate. His father said, "Maybe you shouldn't, Craig. This is a tough business. You have already failed at a lot of things. You have no sales experience. Try something else." Ouch. With that, Craig became a real estate agent. Here's his story about it, in his own words:

"For the first time in my life, I really knuckled down to work. I did what all new agents do—I looked around at what every other agent was doing, copied them, and then outworked them. 18-hour days. Dawn to dark. And I did succeed. Within 36 months, I was the #1 RE/MAX agent in the entire world. But it was clear to me that my financial success was really failure in disguise! I made the radical decision to burn it all down and replace it with a radically different, better approach to the business. That not only produced real success for me, but it is a system I teach to the thousands of other agents, including many made millionaire agents by it, that I coach every month."

Here Are a Few of the Applecarts Craig Proctor Turned Over and Upside Down:

He trashed the typical, pretty, slick brand advertising used by almost all agents and urged on them by all the big companies, including the one he was part of, RE/MAX. He replaced it with direct response lead generation, found, in large part, from me. At the time, this was unprecedented. Today, thanks to Craig's coaching of agents, it is not quite as strange as a dinosaur in a purple tuxedo showing up at your door, but it is still sneered at and largely misunderstood. Because it contradicts what the big companies urge agents to do, Craig is basically *persona non grata* at large industry conventions—so he holds his own. An entire industry of ad agencies, social media agencies, graphics companies, and producers of ordinary, fancy-pants websites have had their work sold to agents put into question. Unlike brand advertising, this can be accurately scored for direct return-on-investment, so we know it pays and pays big. I'm happy to have played a little role in this applecart upsetting.

He created meaningful risk reversal guarantees, like his Guaranteed Sales Program: warranty to sell the client's home in a certain number of days or buy it for a pre-agreed price. Craig first introduced this in the 1980s and it skyrocketed his business but raised the ire of competitors. Questions were raised by jealous competitors angry at losing listings to him about the ethics or legality of the guarantee. Most agents Craig coached were afraid of it, and warmed to it slowly. Today the industry is divided in two: the majority who only promise to sell your house and the minority who back the promise with a written guarantee and their own money.

He stopped and he stopped agents he coaches from the normal, standard, common way of pursuing FSBOs—For Sale By Owners. He was ahead of the Do-Not-Call Law that eventually went into effect in 2006.

He learned to recruit, organize, and manage an effective team, to own and run a real estate agent business, instead of having a bad job just called a business. The industry norm was: Do everything yourself. Craig found out through painful personal experience that even the financially successful solo agent has no life, constantly disappoints his family, is on the edge of burnout constantly, and delivers poor client service by being stretched too thin. Craig invented the team concept in real estate. He was the first agent to build a team *as an agent*, not as a broker.

These are only a few of many Craig Proctor innovations. He says, "Things presented to me as THE RULES turned out not to be rules at all. They were just other people's opinions, paradigms, ignorance, and bad habits!"

Craig has recently retired from his highly successful real estate agent business, a multimillionaire, splitting time between homes in two cities,

and enjoying life. But he continues to coach a group of ultra-high-performing agents and another group of agents with ambition to own great businesses, so he is currently intimately familiar with the changing dynamics and technology of his field. He continues to be a controversial figure by finding ways to break the next rule asserted in the field.

RESOURCE ALERT!

If you are a real estate agent serious about having more income, time, and freedom, visit LessWorkMoreSales.com to see how Craig can help you.

So What About Me?

When I started in speaking, I was told by many never to tell a joke that might offend *anybody* and never to talk about politics, religion, or sex. After a very short time, it dawned on me there wasn't anything of importance left to talk about and, if you never risked telling a joke that might offend somebody, you can't tell a joke, period. If I stuck with that advice, I'd be so bland I'd be invisible. As I've matured as a speaker, I've taken more risks and I've used edgier material. It has only backfired one time in all my decades. Sprinkled throughout my presentations are one-liners and quick shots at liberals, insurance agents, Avon ladies, Jehovah's Witnesses, academics, plumbers, and an assortment of other constituencies often found in my audiences. Every once in a while, somebody complains about being personally offended or about finding me, in general, obnoxious. That's when I know I got it right. Today, the danger of authentic speech, of possibly offensive ideas, of taking any position, has grown to ridiculous levels, thanks to social media gifting every idiot a platform and to the noise of a few magnified to seem like a huge majority. The risks of timidity are greater, though: no attention, no interest, no affinity, no magnetism. I counsel my clients to do their best to operate in friendly territory, but not to neuter themselves out of fear.

Maybe you've noticed: Controversy seems to follow "stars" or standouts in every field. It certainly has followed me. I have clients who swear by me, and critics who swear at me. In the "success" field, as a speaker and an author, titles of my presentations and books—notably *The Ultimate No B.S., No Holds Barred, Kick Butt, Take No Prisoners, and Make Tons of Money Business Success Book* and *No B.S. Ruthless Management of People and Profits*—have sparked controversy. Some have taken the "No B.S." out of context and, with zero sense of humor, used it to accuse me of being offensive to Christians and profane. (Not my intent.) Others have focused on the "tons of money" and been offended by that. And THIS book is certain to offend many of my speaking colleagues, those who make their living by unthinkingly, robotically parroting the same old success dogma. These titles have done their job—attracted the attention and stimulated the interest of the kind of people I want as customers, who are particularly like-minded, and they have repelled people who I do not want attention from at all.

To Be a Chameleon or Not to Be a Chameleon

In recent years, there has been a rush of books, seminars, training programs for salespeople, and the like teaching techniques akin to chameleonism. These suggest altering your entire personality to "match" or "mirror" the person or people you are dealing with at the moment. A little bit of this is useful. There is logic to modifying your selling or communicating "style" to be more acceptable to the other person. But you can certainly carry it too far. Politicians do this to the nth degree, which largely accounts for how little respect anybody has for any of them. If you say, "Will the real <insert politician of your choice> stand up?" there's nobody who can. You may win some temporary victories with this approach, but after changing your colors so many times, will you have any true colors left? The contrarian approach: presenting a consistent personality, being yourself, saying what you mean, meaning what you say, and having everybody know it is more likely to lead to lasting, satisfying success.

In fact, there is abundant proof that a maverick, unconventional, even odd style can lead to success. Nobody should feel required to be somebody or something totally different from what they really are in order to excel. Because I am often blunt, even harsh, I was very pleased at one meeting of executives, at a company I was doing a lot of advisory work for, to overhear its president answer somebody's question about me—why is he here?—with a sigh, saying, "We pay him to annoy us."

How Much More Offensive Can You Be?

The two biggest figures in broadcasting are Howard Stern and the late Rush Limbaugh. I certainly do not need to tell you that Howard Stern offends somebody with almost every word uttered. Howard is thought of as offensive by people who've tuned in and by many who haven't but think they know him by reputation. The exact same thing was true of Rush, although all similarities between the two end with being offensive to a large swath of the public—and being magnetic to a different, big audience.

Rush Limbaugh was fired in 1984 from a Kansas City radio station for delivering overly controversial, conservative commentaries. He got hired by a Sacramento station to replace Morton Downey Jr., and was told by management, "We're not afraid of controversy here. But we will not back you up if you say things you don't believe. If you can convince us why you believe something, no matter how outrageous it seems, we'll back you up all day long. But we will not have controversy just for the sake of it." Rush says that policy stayed with him and forged his career from that point forward. By his own estimate, Rush mightily offended 40 to 50 percent of the people with his current topical, conservative daily broadcasts. And you rarely found anybody who was lukewarm. People either hated or loved Limbaugh. Offending those he offended and winning over those who agreed with him made him a multimillion-dollar media personality with the power to make his own books instant best sellers, to literally "make" little-known products into marketplace giants—like Snapple beverages and UGGs slippers—and some say to have made the Newt Gingrich–Republican takeover of the House in 1995 possible. People who loved him really, really loved him, and mourned his death greatly.

Limbaugh exemplified some of my pet marketing theories: that your ability to create fierce loyalty and enthusiasm for your cause, business, products, or yourself as a personality is restricted only by the extent to which you are willing to create fierce opposition.

CONTRARIAN SUCCESS STRATEGY

If you wait to be discovered and rewarded based on merit alone, you had better bring a lunch and several good books because you're going to be waiting a long, long time. The bigger your ambitions, the more likely you are to offend people while achieving those ambitions. And your opportunity to have meaningful impact will be in direct proportion to your willingness to offend. What others perceive as arrogance may very well be the level of confidence, self-promotion, and pushiness necessary. Also, arrogance magnetically attracts more than it repels because many people prefer association with an individual who is absolutely certain of himself and his convictions.

Leaders in fields, highest income earners, and most prominent figures become that by upsetting applecarts and disrupting the ways things are supposed to be done.

CHAPTER 6

Must You Invent?
A Pox on Creativity

*"I have never made the slightest effort
to compose anything original."*

—*Wolfgang Amadeus Mozart*

W hen I decided to get into the advertising business, I had this mental picture of wild-eyed creative people, some smoking funny cigarettes, in a giant, cluttered, chaotic conference room, shouting out ideas, being creative. It was somewhat of a shock to find out that most effective advertising is not created this way. Actually, the opposite is pretty much true. Some of the smartest, highest-paid strategists I now know in advertising, who come up with famous campaigns you see on TV or in your favorite magazine or in online media, are very organized, disciplined people who amass and consider huge amounts of data and information and finally arrive at their ideas in a very deliberate fashion. Some of these people are even dull!

As I've grown older, however, I've come to appreciate this pedantic approach. And to abhor the "new" or "original" idea. We rarely get paid for any original ideas. We get paid for creating profitable results—and nobody cares if we produced those results by originality and invention or just dogged implementation.

He Is Annoying and He Is a Thief, but He Gets Results

I have dubbed a longtime private client of mine, Parthiv Shah, "my annoying little Indian." He is quite small. He is from India. And he is annoying. I am far from alone in that last judgment. I call him this *affectionately*. Having attention called to him by my pointing him out at seminars from the stage or in my newsletters has brought him a lot of clients and made him a lot of money. I'm afraid he now deliberately tries to annoy me so I won't forget to identify him as MY annoying little Indian. As if.

Parthiv owns several terrific companies, including eLaunchers.com and, specific to dentistry, SellMoreImplants.com. For these companies, he has "stolen" and continues to "steal" my advertising and marketing strategies and devices that work, tweak them to be his, and implement them for his clients. For years he has been glued to me like Velcro, picking up one successful strategy after another, seen deployed in different businesses, making it his, and adding it to the ever-growing portfolio of business tools and systems that his companies customize and manage for many hundreds of clients. It is legal and ethical and smart, as he is careful not to violate copyrights, trademarks or patents, or take verbatim. For example, I have a marketing device that I started using for myself and for clients about 30 years ago, called the shock-and-awe package. It got that name after my speaking colleague General Norm Schwarzkopf's Operation Desert Storm, where he said they went in so big and fast with such overwhelming force they caused shock and awe. Parthiv has made it a component part in the complete marketing system he implements for his clients. He's made over 300 different such packages, all on my architecture, all incorporating what works from my design and content, but so customized for each client that it is fair play. You can see his work with these packages in a seven-minute video at elaunchers.com/shock-awe.

This is not to say that my annoying little Indian has no ingenuity of his own. He does. He even holds U.S. Patent #11,507,967 for his own business growth system. There are only six other patents granted, total, for such things. He can invent. But mostly, he doesn't. Instead, he finds what has been invented and well-proven somewhere, in some field, in some category of enterprise, brings it home, and breeds it with his other strategies and media that work, creating his own iteration.

Parthiv gets to success for his businesses and his clients by massive implementation, not by invention. He is a living representation of Jim Rohn's Principle of *Massive* Action. As an example, he built and tested 450 different marketing funnels using ClickFunnels' preexisting software and online tools. Only 9 of the 450 produced profits. Two of them made him over $1 million and earned him the Two-Comma Award from ClickFunnels. He is also a great data scientist, often assembling and poring through massive amounts of data from within a client's business to find overlooked opportunities to deploy already working systems to—like those two-million-dollar funnels. He utilizes a lot of already existing tools, from companies like HubSpot, Keap, and ClickFunnels. He wastes no time "reinventing the wheel."

"The myth," Parthiv says, "is that you must invent something brand new, make a new breakthrough product, be creative. That can be exciting, but it is just not necessary. More fortunes are made by implementation than by invention. I am the guy who implements for my clients. I am the guy who automates implementation. The truth is, nothing needs to be original to you because most people have lots of ideas, including some good ones, but are very poor at implementation and follow-through. You can succeed by doing what they never get done."

RESOURCE ALERT!

You can see Parthiv's bookshelf and access free books at Free-MarketingBooks.com and watch a free video about business growth at elaunchers.com/it-takes-a-village.

The Incredible Power of Doing the Ordinary Well

A onetime client of mine in Dayton, Ohio, Marty Grunder, started a little business while going to college; he mowed lawns. He started out with one piece of equipment (a lawn mower), one employee (himself), and one simple marketing plan—he would ask people if they wanted their lawns mowed and, if they said yes, he would do an exemplary job, then offer a continuing contract. Shortly after he graduated and went full-time, his business did well over a million dollars in sales. His company expanded to doing everything from the simple mowing of lawns to complex landscaping projects for businesses as well as homes. In the winter, they plowed snow out of driveways and parking lots. In a very short period of time, Marty's company became the biggest and best-known landscaping company in southern Ohio.

He didn't "create" anything, he studied the customer service and customer satisfaction principles and techniques used by the companies in other businesses with the most loyal customers—like Nordstrom, Ritz-Carlton—and copied those that he could. He insisted that everybody on his team be neatly attired in uniforms, that trucks and equipment be kept clean, that scheduled appointments be honored. He collected newsletters used by other businesses, then put together a similar customer newsletter of his own. Marty's business was very ordinary. He did not have any superior technology, new inventions, or innovative advantages. He did fundamental things very well. And got rich doing them.

Whenever I talk with people about this, I point out Fred DeLuca's Subway chain. Is there anything more *basic* than a sub sandwich? Fred understood the magic of simplicity. While much of the fast-food industry wrestles with saturation issues, Subway franchises are proliferating like burger joints did in the 1950s. He opened his first store in 1965, at age seventeen, with a $1,000 loan. Now the Subway chain is second in number of outlets only to McDonald's, although much younger than McDonald's, and the race is on. And Subway doesn't even have its own "special sauce." Something simple, ordinary, and uncreative: fresh cold cuts and toppings, fresh-baked rolls, convenient locations, and straightforward, product-driven advertising. Nothing here that any of thousands of independent mom-and-pop sub shop owners couldn't have done to turn their tiny businesses into global empires. No creativity required.

Chipotle, incidentally, *is* Subway.

You Need Only *One* Creative Thought to Get Rich; Two Just About Guarantees It

My friend the late E. Joseph Cossman became quite famous in the world of marketing as the man who found one nearly dead or lazy product after another, inventions that never blossomed, bought certain distribution rights to them—often for very small sums in advance of royalties—and then made millions with each one. One right after another after another. In none of these big wins was new invention involved. Mostly, Joe had one creative thought about each one, seeing a different market or advertising and sales method for the product. I teach this as Place Strategy: moving a product to a different, un-obvious place of far greater opportunity than its present, obvious place. Joe's biggest success at this was with The Ant Farm. When he spotted it, it sold in very modest numbers, only through school supply houses, for use in biology classrooms.

Joe intuitively felt that little boys would be fascinated watching the ants tunnel and work in this flat-screen aquarium, at home, in their rooms, and get a kick out of their mothers *not* liking it. This changed its market size from all the schools to all the preteen boys. That's a gigantic change! He implemented his idea with full-page mail-order ads placed in comic books. He immediately had a blockbuster success on his hands. With the fantastic results of his ads as proof, he was able to get every toy store and major mass retailer to stock the product. The Ant Farm continues to sell today, decades after Joe moved it.

Richard Thalheimer, the founder of The Sharper Image, was inspired by Joe Cossman. Richard was adept at taking already-existing, slow-moving, utilitarian products and repositioning them as amazing inventions; gadgets you just had to have. Today's Sharper Image mail-order catalog and e-commerce business owes much to what Richard learned observing Joe Cossman. My friend Joe Sugarman was also inspired by Joe Cossman. Joe Sugarman took the ordinary desktop calculator, got a smaller-sized one made, and was the first marketer to offer it, as an amazing new technological breakthrough, in full-page ads in all the airlines' seat-pocket magazines. He later had his biggest success with an ordinary product widely available: sunglasses. He had his manufactured with a special tint, named them BluBlockers®, advertised them in half-hour TV infomercials featuring man-on-the-street demonstrations, sold them on home shopping channels, and ultimately rolled them out to retail distribution. BluBlockers® made Joe Sugarman a big fortune. This type of sunglass was not his invention. Sunglasses tinted to screen out harmful rays, sharpen vision, and improve night vision had already been put into the marketplace, but were never mass-advertised, and were poorly sold through opticians' offices.

If these guys interest you, if you'll check Amazon by their names, you'll find books written by them or about them.

In the 1970s, microwaves were big, bulky things sold only to restaurants. Some executives at a manufacturer of then, Litton Industries, had the crazy idea that people would want microwave ovens in their homes. Ignoring the laughter, they advertised for independent sales agents to sell the ovens door-to-door and at home parties, like Tupperware® parties. The success led to quickly designing a smaller, less bulky, less powerful, and more affordable microwave fit for the home, and the rest is history. You've got one in your home. So does everybody else.

A more contemporary example, a favorite of mine, is Steve Jobs's one creative idea: Similar to the microwave being sold only to restaurants, computers were sold only to businesses. Jobs saw it in the home. He had a second, linked creative idea that was really "out there": to have his own retail stores selling only his computers. At the mall, wedged in between Victoria's Secret and Mr. Pretzel, a big Apple computer store! The entire industry laughed.

How, you might ask, can this be applied to small business? I often tell the story of the jewelry store owner who opened a pop-up store at the racehorse auctions I often attend. Every other vendor there sells horse "stuff": equipment, race sulkies, liniment. He is a fish out of water. But, when John promised his wife he was not going to buy another horse, but does, bringing home a diamond tennis bracelet with the new horse helps. The jewelry retailer has his pop-up store at every auction. He tells me he can do as much business there in two days as in two weeks in his mall stores, and with no discounting. Did he invent anything? No. Pop-up stores already existed. They were common. Vendors renting exhibit space at all sorts of events already existed. His jewelry store already existed. He just had one great creative idea, worth a fortune.

If you happen to be the kind of person who births revolutionary breakthrough ideas, you'd better face up to the reality of having to shelve the thinking cap, put on the work clothes, roll up your sleeves, and do a lot of uncreative, unfun work to turn it into something of value. If you are the kind of person who thinks you never have new ideas and haven't got a single creative gene in your DNA, you ought to take comfort in knowing that ideas alone are like unplanted seeds. What you can bring to the table can be much more important. Certainly creativity is not required to create extraordinary business or financial success.

But It Goes Beyond "No Creativity Required"; Creativity Can Even Get in the Way of Success!

Back to me and the advertising business. And the secret of the "swipe file." Although I get paid very large amounts of money to "create" ads, sales letters, and other media for my clients, I really am not a very creative person—whatever that is—and I do my best to rein in what creative impulses I do have, because clients are much better served by my copying and piecing together already proven "stuff" than by my indulging my creativity. Here's how world-class direct response advertising is REALLY "created": When I get a new client, I first want to get my hands on everything he's done and the results, and everything his competitors have done that they've continued doing long enough that you can reasonably conclude it is effective. From this, I want to preserve and recycle the most useful ideas, themes, copy, offers, and NOT throw everything out and "create" anew, just to demonstrate my ingenuity or to feed my ego. Second, I go to my "swipe files." For example, I have files of "great (proven) headlines" divided up by category—for example, headlines for consumer offers, headlines for business-to-business offers, headlines emphasizing guarantees, headlines emphasizing new breakthroughs, etc., etc. From these files, I choose several headlines than can work for my client. Then I go to my swipe files of offers. And my swipe files of story copy. And so on. Eventually, I have puzzle pieces that I can put in order and that provide the foundation and raw material for an ad or sales letter. Then I smooth it all out. Make the pieces connect. Change words, phrases, terminology to fit the client's products and customers. I wind up with an ad that has mostly written itself out of "old," used material. This is not invention. It's implementation.

Now, to be 100 percent honest, I've been doing so much of this for so long that I have some very big swipe files stored in my subconscious, and I can often work with those, without actually, physically raiding the file cabinets in the corner. But the process is the same. The method is the same: stitching together already tested, proven, effective material, NOT creating anything from scratch.

Incidentally, I'm NOT suggesting copyright infringement or outright theft of protected intellectual property. Every good copywriter has a "swipe file" and uses that slang term to describe it—but what we mean is borrowing, combining, integrating, and modifying (rather than creating), so that our new whole is sufficiently different from any of the parts so as not to violate any laws or ethical considerations. However, there are very formulaic approaches to good advertising. For example, there's a very famous, no longer copyright-protected headline originally written by John Caples over sixty years ago: "They Laughed When I Sat Down at the Piano—But When I Started to Play." This has been, and should be, much copied over the years. For example, one of my own borrowings: "Everybody Laughed When I Said I'd Never Work for Somebody Else Again—but I Sure Had the Last Laugh. My Story of Financial Freedom Could Become Yours, Too. Here's How." This headline was for a very successful direct-mail campaign I put together for a client selling home-based business information.

Anyway, in the advertising business, I all too often see creativity for creativity's sake being put ahead of the clients' interests or the desire for results. Worshiping at the altar of creativity blinds people to easier, more straightforward, less risky opportunities. Overrating the importance of creativity holds many people back from pursuing opportunity.

Sometimes creativity backfires.

There's a very big, long-established U.S. company I'm not going to name here that had the same famous logo for over 50 years. When a new president came in, he was looking around for things to change—I think to sort of stake out his territory and demonstrate his authority, the way an animal stakes out his territory by urinating on its border. He brought all the internal marketing folks and his ad agency people together and told them the company had to "get with it," get a new, more modern image. After over a million dollars invested in this creative exercise, the old logo was jettisoned and a new logo was introduced. The old one, by the way, clearly identified the company's product. The new one showed only the corporate name in a very fashionable, difficult-to-read type style. Logos were torn down and replaced on hundreds of stores nationwide; catalogs, brochures, and other literature and websites were transformed, and the company launched an advertising campaign doing nothing but advertising the new corporate logo.

The public reacted, well, by at first not reacting at all. It was a "who cares?" for the consumer. Then, as enough time passed to measure change in market share, the new logo proved to be hurting rather than helping sales. After a number of months, the company's wizards gave in and redesigned the new logo to incorporate the old logo. And that half-breed logo has "stuck" for the last 20 years.

A giant, costly, creative exercise launched by whim, rejected by the public.

At the time I was writing this, a new, young, very creative marketing executive decided that Bud® and Bud Light® were stuck in misogynistic, toxic male, non-inclusive images and humor and that she needed to "shake things up." She did an ad on YouTube featuring a popular, transgender YouTube personality. Sales plummeted. Bars dropped Bud Light® from their taps. Boycotts were organized. Kid Rock made a YouTube video of himself blasting away at a Bud Light® can with an AK-47, which got millions of views. In revenue and stock value, her creative misadventure cost some $40 billion. That's a lot of cans of beer. In baseball, it's called an unforced error. The Bud Light® customer base making it the best-selling light beer had not, in any way, indicated boredom or disapproval toward its advertising nor, I'm confident, was there research and careful testing to support her creative and radical ideas. The customer was grossly misunderstood. Maybe disdained. And a very, very big price was paid.

God Forbid, We Should Do What Works

At a seminar I did on using certain direct response marketing strategies for agent recruiting in the insurance industry, I started out by introducing "models" and asking: Who is already effectively, efficiently, and very successfully recruiting exactly the kind of people you want but can't seem to get? In this case, the answers are, one, the business opportunity/franchise industry, and two, the network or multilevel marketing industry. For the latter, I used the biggest success, Amway Corporation, as the number one "model" to learn from. But one executive from one of the insurance companies was mightily offended by this reference. Comparing her prestigious, professional company to Amway was an insult! This executive couldn't keep ego and emotion, the twin enemies of logic, out of the way for even a few minutes.

In this case, any of tens of thousands of moderately successful Amway distributors, relative amateurs with modest budgets, recruit more high-income, white-collar professionals in a month than this entire giant insurance corporation does in two years, spending ten times the amount per recruit to get the job done. But God forbid we should try to figure out how those unprofessional, lowly Amway people do that and what we can borrow from them to reach our desired results!

In my experience, for every marketing challenge, for every entrepreneurial objective, for every personal desire, there is somewhere at least one successful model that already has plenty of answers available to anybody willing to pay attention. Solving problems does not require creative invention. It requires solutions.

The Biggest Copycats Work in One of the Most "Creative" Industries of All

In Hollywood, very little money is made from true creativity, but a whole lot of money is made from putting old wine in a new bottle.

Turn on the tube. *The Jetsons* were *The Flintstones* transplanted to outer space. *Star Wars* was all the old Westerns transplanted to outer space. Today, Netflix and Amazon Prime are loaded to the gills with old and very old TV series and films a lot of people never saw, and at least half of its "new" content comes from outright remakes of shows or movies already done two or three times. Old movies are turned into new, spin-off TV series like, as I write this, *True Lies, American Idol*, and *AGT: America's Got Talent*. These shows are all do-overs of classic talent competition programs swiping from the very dawn of black-and-white TV. The last truly original idea to come out of Hollywood may have been the big sign up on the hill overlooking the city. And that's okay. It's *a business*. About sales, ad revenue, viewer numbers, streaming subscription revenue. About profit. Trying to raise the likelihood of a success by greatly borrowing from prior successes is just good business.

Why risk creating from scratch when there are so many fantastic models to copy from? This is the network or studio CEO's smart question, as he tries to prudently invest partners' and stockholders' capital. I suggest it as a very smart question for you, too.

CONTRARIAN SUCCESS STRATEGY

Forget all about "creativity" as it is commonly perceived and understood. If you feel like you haven't got a creative bone in your body, you can stop worrying about that, because it clearly does not matter. In fact, even creative folks need to fight creativity for creativity's sake and focus instead on doing what has already proven itself, a bit better. Never underestimate the value and power of the ordinary implemented with extraordinary zeal and diligence.

CHAPTER 7

Forget (Almost) Everything You've Ever Been Told About Persistence

"If at first you don't succeed, try, try again.
Then quit. There's no use being a damn fool about it."

—*W. C. Fields*

P ersistence is vastly overrated. You have undoubtedly been lectured to about persistence. *Just keep trying. Try harder.* If you've bought into this, you've probably also suffered a tremendous amount of frustration and guilt. Because of this "persist at all costs" ethic, those who "quit" often equate that with "being a loser" and lug around that guilt and despair everywhere they go.

It's a harmful ethic. We've actually wound up glorifying the virtue of doing things the hard way, even if an easier path is present, and for doing the hardest thing, even when an easier thing would accomplish the same objective. The American Way became the hard way.

I would like to redirect you to accomplishing your goals in the easiest way possible. I like shortcuts. I favor getting things done the easy way. If you can get the desired result while lying in a hammock under a shade tree, sipping lemonade, and talking on your cellular phone while someone else pursues the same objectives by fighting traffic, dragging an overstuffed briefcase up and down the street, and sitting in waiting rooms watching time tick-tock away, I applaud you. That is not a blanket endorsement of the Work from Home Movement, nor of working remotely. Isolation kills collaboration, prohibits discovery, shrinks productivity for most people, and, generally, makes Jack a dull boy. However, there's no great virtue in showing up anywhere for work toward goals and purposes, and persisting with unnecessarily difficult methods.

Don't misunderstand. I abhor sloth. I detest those who want or take something for nothing. I believe in the value of work. I just don't think there's extra gold stars to be had from climbing a mountain when an elevator's waiting nearby.

Proof That Sheer Persistence Isn't the Answer to All the Questions

The sales manager's most frequent answer to the frustrated salesman is, "Make more calls." The parent's answer to the struggling student is, "Study harder." But there's a flaw in all this. Once I said to a golf expert, "Maybe I just need to practice more." "Not if you practice THAT swing," he said.

Let me give you a couple examples to demonstrate how most people persist foolishly.

For about a decade, I did a lot of work in the television infomercial business—you know, those annoying half-hour programs that sell you spray paint for your bald head, wrinkle creams, and success courses. I've worked with countless celebrities. This is a, very high-risk, very high-reward business. The typical infomercial requires $100,000 to $500,000 or even more to produce, and that's before buying the first minute of airtime. The success rate is only about 1 in 15. And here's the quirky part: After investing $250,000 in putting an infomercial together, a $20,000 test, over a single weekend, tells its tale. You know right then and there whether or not it is driving enough people to the phones to order the advertised product.

If it is not making the phone ring, spending another $100,000 airing it some more will NOT change the results. But the way most people view and define "persistence," they would do just that: keep running the same unsuccessful show over and over again, somehow expecting the results to change thanks to sheer persistence. Won't happen.

You Can Whip a Horse Harder, but You Still Can't Make Him Win

As a kid, I grew up around harness racing. I returned to it after a 20-year hiatus, as an adult, and built up a sizable stable, and even drove professionally in races for 20 years. A Standardbred, a harness horse, trotter, or pacer, but particularly a pacer, is a complex animal. A pacer has dozens of different types of equipment to possibly help it race better: hobbles set at different lengths, knee boots, ankle boots, head poles, blinders, different bridle bits, and so on. The blacksmith can give it different types of horseshoes, tilt and weight the shoes differently, put extra grips on or take them off. Every one of those variables can alter the horse's performance. I learned that as soon as you determine the horse is performing unsatisfactorily, you start experimenting. Systematically, you try out one change at a time. Blinders on—then what happens? Blinders off—what happens? Cotton in the ears—what happens? And so on. With this, you persist methodically until you have exhausted the possibilities. Then, you quit. You find a new home for the horse.

But this is not how most people persist. They would just keep racing that horse "as is," probably whipping his butt a little harder each time, trying to change the results through sheer persistence. Won't happen.

Most people would want that darned horse to try harder.

But if that horse has the wrong shoes on, it won't matter how hard he tries. Trying harder won't help. Only getting the right shoes can help.

A racehorse MUST rest one to three days after each race. He literally leaves his heart out there on the track. Tries as hard as he can. Telling a racehorse to "just try harder" is dumb. Finding ways to free up his peak performance is smart.

Attention, managers, coaches, parents: Just telling 'em to try harder is dumb. Finding ways to free up their peak performance is smart. That reminds me of failing geography in high school. Well, I was failing it. But my parents went out and bought me a globe and a book on how to more easily memorize and remember things like lists. They didn't just yell "study harder!"; they did what they could to make it possible for me to study more effectively. I brought that F up to a C.

Some businesses persist with losing plans. In the year or so of this book's writing and a few years before, big retail chains like Borders bookstores and Bed Bath & Beyond died. During the Virus lockdowns, quite a few restaurants and shops died. Up against Walmart or Amazon, retailers have died. Yet in the same time periods and conditions, other nearly identical businesses creatively adapted, survived, even thrived. What separates the dead from the living? It *isn't* simple persistence.

In Chapter 5, you read about my client Craig Proctor who achieved huge success largely through hard work and sheer persistence only to realize it was unsustainable. He stopped persisting with the methods that got him to the top and reengineered everything, creatively, more cleverly.

In simple terms, persistence should be deserved, not just indiscriminately given.

Anyway, most people's ideas about persistence are just a step away from watching the "instant replay," hoping your horse that just finished fifth comes in first in the replay. He won't. Ever.

Is "Sticking to Your Game Plan" an Admirable Trait of a Tough-Minded Leader OR...

Coaches lose plenty of games this way. You see them on TV, coming out of the locker room after halftime, their team down by 28 points, their players beat up and befuddled, and the coach growls to the TV commentator: "We're gonna stick to our game plan." What?!? Haven't you been paying attention? Your game plan ain't working, man! Your guys are getting their butts kicked up and down the field. "We're gonna stick to our game plan." This is not persistence. This is stupidity. Oh, and the next thing this coach'll say is: "Our guys just have to try harder."

How a Restaurant Owner Persisted, All the Way to Bankruptcy

Some years ago, I had some friends who were slowly, painfully going broke in the restaurant business. When I dropped by to see them, here's how their end of the conversation usually went:

Well, we're at the end of our rope, but we're going to tie a knot in the end and hold on! We're going to tough it out. Winners never quit and quitters never win, you know.

And they did tough it out. They kept showing up every day at the same time, doing the same things, and moving inches closer to bankruptcy. When the time came that they couldn't pay their suppliers with inspirational sayings, they closed the door and slunk away. "When the going gets tough, the tough get going"—in this case, right out of business, right out of town.

There were different things they could have done. They might have introduced a lunch and meeting catering service to all the area companies. They might have gotten on the phone and called all their past customers that seemed "lost," inviting them back in with a special offer. They might have created a membership program for their loyalists and re-capitalized the business with the up-front payments. They might have found a nearby busy business, like the giant car wash a few miles away, and persuaded them to give out BOGO coupons as customer gifts. The *No B.S. Grassroots Marketing* guide, that I co-authored with Jeff Slutsky, features these kinds of strategies. There is no way to know if any or all of these actions might have stopped and reversed their slide into the abyss. But one thing is certain: Persistence with what they were doing wasn't going to. If it would, it would already have.

It is vital to be ferociously committed to and persistent with your purpose but relatively open-minded, creative, and adaptive about your modus operandi.

Jeff Bezos originally thought he was going to be in the online bookstore business, permanently. Walt Disney's team thought they were getting into the amusement park business, and even Walt thought Disney World would pull visitors only from adjacent states who traveled there by car, many needing campgrounds. I initially thought I was in the speaking business, but I quickly understood it was a terrible business but a very good media and method for acquiring customers in clumps, to feed into *something*, and I created that something.

How a Salesman Used Persistence to Ruin His Career

I once watched a salesman slowly destroy his career by accumulating, babying, and finally being buried in "maybes." He manipulated every contact and conversation so that the prospect gave him, and kept giving him, "maybe" as his answer. He had a desk drawer full to overflowing with three-by-five cards of "maybes." And he took great pride in his persistent contact with these prospects, month after month after month.

Unfortunately for him, his much-prized persistence had no real-world value. The highest income earners in sales move as quickly as possible to get a definite yes *OR* a definite no. Getting a definite no frees them from investing any more time or energy in that prospect and spurs them on to the next. Speed of getting through noes automatically guarantees more yeses.

The salesman who destroyed his career devoutly believed that if he persisted in contacting these prospects again and again and again, he would eventually get business from them through sheer persistence. He believed that his persistence alone would eventually break down whatever resistance the prospects had.

He was sadly misled and mistaken on two counts. First, selling should be preceded by smart and sophisticated marketing that separates the valid, viable prospects from the rest, so that the salesman can be more efficient. He'll automatically get more yeses. This is one of the purposes my Magnetic Marketing System® serves—which I invented out of necessity way back when I was a salesman. Second, he had become convinced that indiscriminate persistence was so virtuous, it had to be rewarded. But persisting in planting seeds in utterly unfertile ground again and again is not going to be rewarded by Mother Nature.

What Thomas Edison Told Napoleon Hill About Persistence

The late Napoleon Hill, author of the famous book *Think and Grow Rich*, visited Thomas Edison in his laboratory. Edison had tried 10,000 times to make electric light work before finally getting it right. Hill asked Edison, "What would you be doing now if your ten thousandth experiment had failed?"

"I would not be standing here talking to you," Edison replied sharply. "I would be locked in my laboratory conducting the next experiment."

This little story is used by lots of motivational speakers as an example of exceptional persistence in action. "Every time you flick on the lights, you can be grateful that Edison was an extraordinarily persistent man," so the story is told. I say: nuts. Every time we flick on the lights, we can be grateful that Edison was a scientist who took a solidly scientific approach to invention. What Napoleon Hill never spelled out, probably assuming people would figure it out for themselves, is that Edison did NOT do the same experiment 10,000 times. He did 10,000 different experiments. He tested 10,000 *different* hypotheses, and he *gave up on* each one as rapidly as possible. He was a "quitter" 10,000 times.

Michael Huang, referenced elsewhere in this book, a leading martial arts thought-leader, gave me this quote: "Remember that the Master has failed more times than the beginner even tried." Failing is never the real problem. It's how you have designed and are doing the failing that matters.

The Breakthrough Success Strategy:
Forget About Persistence; Think "Testing"

For the past 40+ years, I've worked in direct response advertising and direct marketing. I want to tell you about what I do for a living in some detail so you can pull a breakthrough strategy for yourself out of how I do business.

Consider a full-page direct response ad or its equivalent as online media, selling some product. You might see such an ad in your daily newspaper, *USA Today*, *National Enquirer*, or a sophisticated business magazine like *Forbes*. You might see it as a website leading into an online funnel, like those facilitated by ClickFunnels. To write such an ad for a client, I'm typically paid $25,000 to $50,000 plus usage royalties. I know that sounds like a great deal of money for writing one ad. I won't bore you with all the research, preparation, and experience that goes into the making of that ad and, in part, justifies my fee. But I will tell you that it is rare for such an ad to be a big success the first time out of the gate. Instead, we often have to do some testing to finally get to the most productive version of the ad. Here are just a few of the variables that can be tested in such an ad:

1. One headline against another.
2. Photograph(s) vs. no photograph(s).
3. One photo caption vs. another.
4. One testimonial vs. a different testimonial.
5. One price vs. another.
6. Single payment vs. "two payments of…"
7. One bonus vs. another.

Then, with all that testing done, the outcome is, hopefully, an ad that can run repetitively at a profit. We call that a "control." And as soon as a "control" is in place, the work begins on a new ad that may be able to beat the control. With it, split-testing starts all over again.

Throughout this entire process, most of the variables tested fail to make any significant difference. Most of the ads tested against the control fail to outperform it.

How often does a skilled, experienced, top pro copywriter develop a winning, lucrative direct response ad? Maybe one out of every four or five attempts. Or worse. In my business, we live with failure every day of our lives, and we must exhibit great patience and persistence—but it has to be the right kind of persistence—that applies to testing and giving up on one hypothesis after another.

Practice Makes Perfect—*NOT!*

You've been told all your life that "practice makes perfect." What a magnificent lie that is.

Earlier I mentioned my golf swing. You should see my natural swing. My picture's posted in golf courses all across the country like criminals' pictures are put up in post offices. Be on the lookout for this guy. With a golf club, he's armed and dangerous. My swing approximates that of a large barn door, clinging to the barn by one rusty hinge, in a windstorm. On my scorecard, there's no place to count strokes. I count hours. It was astutely pointed out to me that if I go out to the driving range and practice that swing, I will only succeed at more deeply embedding that swing into my psyche and muscle memory. Persistence with it is my worst enemy. That seems obvious, but how often, in how many different situations, are we telling ourselves or others to engage in exactly that kind of persistence?

If the salesman who cannot close a sale sits down in front of a mirror for two hours a day and practices, even memorizes his presentation, what will the result be? His ineffective presentation will be more firmly locked in. He will be better than ever at failing to close sales.

No, practice does not make perfect.

But let's take our struggling salesman and teach him a highly effective presentation, including techniques known to close a very high percentage of the time. Then we have him deliver that presentation and we videotape it. Then we play it back, coaching him on what he did well, what he did not do so well, and how he can improve. Then he delivers it again, we videotape again, we coach again. When he finally owns this effective presentation, he practices using it on his own, in his imagination, running and rerunning a vivid "mental movie" of himself delivering the presentation and securing orders. (This "mental movie" technique is borrowed from Psycho-Cybernetics. This is how dentists master case presentations. How lawyers assemble closing arguments.)

Some years ago, we used this kind of practice, video role-play, and so on to help hundreds of doctors of chiropractic improve their reports of findings and other presentations to patients. In some instances, doctors as much as doubled the percentage of new patients accepting their treatment programs. Doctors' incomes as much as doubled from one month to the next.

Where Did These Erroneous Ideas About Persistence Come From, Anyway?

Much of what is repeatedly taught about persistence traces back to very different times. Times when a person went to school, then served a couple years' apprenticeship under a "master," then ever so slowly worked his way up a vertical ladder in a single career, vocation, or business. Times when a person got a job with a good company, stayed there for 40 years, and retired. You got on one track and stayed on that track. Plodding, mostly, not racing.

You may argue whether it is good, bad, better, or worse, but this is not the way the world works today.

I never saw my father make an easy dollar in his life. I learned "work ethic" from him, for which I'm grateful, because it is useful and, these days, rare. But it is not a panacea. And I also developed a tendency to try and accomplish my goals by outworking everybody else on the planet. Gradually, I discovered that pure, unmitigated, dogged persistence has very little real-world value but often has very high real-world cost. I learned that just one tap applied at just the right place, at just the right time, is more powerful than hammering away blindly, clumsily, and stubbornly.

Persistence as a virtue comes from Calvinist religion. Like a lot of dogma, it was and is without nuance. Raising questions about "persisting at what?" complicates what dogma demands be a simple, bumper sticker–length commandment. I tell people: Don't step in dogma! Success requires a more sophisticated navigation. Persistence has to be applied where it can do good but cast aside where it does harm.

Consider this "easy versus hard" scenario:

Tom H. is a new stockbroker. Like all new brokers, he is handed a directory of some sort, a list of tired leads, aimed at his friends, family, and college alumni, given a phone, and told to have at it. If he struggles, he's told to make more calls. If he has superhuman persistence to make hundreds of calls a day, absorb massive amounts of rejection, struggle mightily to get a new client, and survive months of starvation, then the other new brokers who started when he started will fall by the wayside, he will gradually gain favor with his superiors, and finally start sharing in better quality leads. But he will be expected to prove his value through dogged, grinding, persistent effort in an antiquated, unrewarding selling environment. If he survives, he will be applauded for his persistence.

This strikes me as remarkably dumb on everybody's part.

Let's suppose that, for Tom, the new broker, I devise a nifty little marketing system that is driven by small, inexpensive print and online ads, and simple sales letters, so Tom never again picks up the phone to make a "cold call." Instead, he only talks to prospects who have taken the initiative of calling him, have qualified themselves via questions in the letter, and are somewhat predisposed to doing business with him. He is now much more productive and much less subject to burn out. Is Tom any "less of a man" because he takes this easier, more efficient, and more effective way?

In the eyes of many, he WOULD be viewed negatively by jealous peers and confused superiors.

Let's take this a step further. With one of my clients, we tested—note that word: "tested"—three different new products and new ad campaigns. One of the three provided instant, terrific results. Another provided mildly encouraging results. The third, very disappointing results.

It so happens that I have the skills and the client has the resources to turn the second one from mediocre to profitable, maybe even to resuscitate the third one. By doing all the things I described earlier that we do in direct response advertising, by testing one variable after another, by fixing, fixing, fixing, I could, eventually, turn either one of those disappointments into profitable campaigns. I might have to invest sizable sums of my client's money. I would be bloodied, bruised, and exhausted. But I could eventually triumph and have a great "war story" to tell.

I didn't do that. I cheerfully threw the two nonperformers right into the trash and forgot all about them as quickly as possible. What I did was zero in on the one that was a standout winner. I gave it all the resources and attention, turned it on "full speed ahead!" and the result was that we made a great deal of easy money. We found ways to "run the winner" in dozens of different "races" (media) instead of working at getting the slow ones to get better.

Does Money Care Whether It Comes to You Easily or Only After Great Difficulty and Mighty Struggle?

When I go to the bank to make a deposit, nobody asks me: Is this easy money or hard-earned money? The bank does not give me a bonus when I deposit hard-earned, hard-fought-for money. The bank does not penalize me for depositing money made easily. The bank doesn't care.

What Is "Quitting"?

"Winners never quit and quitters never win"—right?

Consider the guy who sets out to learn how to play golf, a difficult game at best. He's going to spend a lot of money on equipment, gadgets, gurus, and practice sessions. He's going to chuck some expensive clubs into the pond. He's going to be frustrated a lot. If his objective, his over-riding goal, really is to become a good golfer, maybe to play with a group of friends, then all that's well and good and necessary, and he is going to need a bundle of persistence to get the job done.

But if his objective is to get some exercise a couple times a week, to drop a few pounds and keep 'em off, and feel better, he might be better off forgetting about golf and taking brisk walks through his neighborhood. If he comes to this realization after a month or two of "fighting" with golf, quits golf, and takes up walking, what does this say about him? Is he a "quitter" with "no persistence"? Or is he just smart? Is he a "winner" or a "loser"?

Setting goals is, generally speaking, a productive thing to do. Certainly, having a vision of where you want to go in life is important. But too often, people get too nitpicky in micro-defining how they'll get there, thus excluding all sorts of great opportunities and sticking themselves with having to summon up huge amounts of persistence to get a goal the hard way even if an easier path presents itself.

Since I was a kid, one of the things I wanted to do was be a writer. Early on, I got hooked on mystery novels. I admire the work of the late Rex Stout and John MacDonald and Robert Parker and John Grisham. For a while, I really worked at writing mysteries. I submitted over 50 different mystery stories to the two major mystery magazines, *Ellery Queen's* and *Alfred Hitchcock's,* and I have 50 rejection slips to prove it. I guess I could have locked myself in a loft and lived on scraps while I kept writing mysteries, and maybe, thanks to incredible persistence, I would eventually have made one work. But maybe not. I have my doubts. I might very well have spent my whole life driving a cab or clerking in a convenience store just to pay the bills while writing mountains of stories no one would publish.

Fortunately, I think, I did not require myself to succeed at writing mysteries. After what I felt was sufficient testing—there's that word "testing" again—I quit trying and moved on to a different type of writing that proved much easier for me. And I was able to do it without feeling like a failure. It turns out that I am remarkably prolific and reasonably talented at writing two things: one, nonfiction, how-to books, newsletters, and related products dealing with business and self-improvement; and two, direct response advertising copy for ads, sales letters, brochures, catalogs, and online media. I routinely get fees of $50,000 to $100,000 or more, plus royalties tied to results, to write direct response materials for interesting clients in dozens of different fields, all over the continent. Doing that made me wealthy. It has also made me influential and popular with an audience of small business owners, entrepreneurs, and sales professionals. Yes, it took SOME persistence to get this writing career going. But frankly, not much, because I found what was easy for me to do and did that.

As a punch line to the story, many years after quitting trying to write and publish mystery novels, wealthy and able to indulge myself, I paid a fee to be "second chair" with a well-established author of dozens of novels in a mystery series, Les Roberts. We then did two books together, each set in one of my worlds: *Speaking of Murder* and *Win, Place, or Die.* I got two mystery novels published, to which I contributed as a co-author. I scratched my itch. Inked off a bucket list item. Without living in a garret on crusts of bread.

Quitters Win a Lot

My friend Mark Victor Hansen failed miserably in business. His construction business went bust. He went bankrupt. And he quit the entire industry.

Most people would prefer hearing the inspiring story of how he went back into that business, started over, clawed his way up, and finally succeeded in a big way. If it took his entire life to do it, it'd be a marvelous story of persistence. And there are stories like that. Mark's just isn't one of them.

He quit the industry entirely, turned his back on everything he knew and had studied (with the famous Buckminster Fuller), on all his experience, and decided to try an entirely different field. He quickly discovered he had a special knack and love for public speaking. He soon found this to be the easiest way he had ever seen to make good money. Over time, he developed into one of the leading inspirational speakers. This led to his biggest success breakthrough: envisioning the book series *Chicken Soup for the Soul*. There are dozens of different titles, each matched to a niche audience. Combined, tens of millions of copies have been sold. The Chicken Soup for the Soul books have held positions on the *New York Times* best-seller list, been translated and published in dozens of countries, created a TV series, and more. In its time, it lifted Mark, making him much more sought after and much better paid as a speaker. Mark has become independently wealthy. But you might call him a quitter.

Getting *Chicken Soup for the Soul* underway required considerable persistence. Mark, and his partner, Jack Canfield, were rejected by every book publisher, only getting a deal, finally, with a small publisher of health books. They sacrificed a lot of income to give days to promoting and getting publicity for the books. The phenomenal success they made is a story of persistence—but persistence poured into something rewarding it. In Mark's case, he had to quit something to find something worthy of his persistence.

The Award I'm Not Sure I Want

In 2013, I was awarded the Napoleon Hill Foundation's Award for Persistence. It was given in recognition of my record of great persistence against many adversities to wind up a shining success earning the right to opine on it, in the *Think and Grow Rich* tradition. It was and is an honor. I display the plaque. But if I had been at a big banquet receiving it and then making acceptance remarks, I would have had to express mixed emotions. I would have said how much I appreciated the honor, but I would have had to denounce the idea of persistence per se being my chief method of success. I would have had to say that persistence applied to viable opportunities and matched with intelligent, sophisticated, multifaceted success methodology was, if you will, my secret—but squeezing all that onto a plaque is problematic.

CONTRARIAN SUCCESS STRATEGY

Be wary of the "quitter" label. Rethink your ideas about goals, persistence, success, and failure. Focus on "testing." And look for that which is easiest, most effective, and most efficient for you to do that can take you in the direction you want to go. If you have diligently tested a plan, product, service, business, etc. and found it unrewarding, it is perfectly okay to bury it in the backyard and move onto a different opportunity or method.

Charlie Munger, Warren Buffett's partner, says they have on their desk an IN BOX, an OUT BOX, and a third TOO DIFFICULT FOR US BOX. If it's okay for two of the world's smartest and most successful investors to admit something is too difficult for them, it's okay for you, too.

CHAPTER 8

"What's Luck Got to Do with It?"

"You've got to place a bet every day; otherwise, you might be walking around lucky and not know it."

—Character played by Richard Dreyfuss in the movie Let It Ride

O n a pleasant May morning in 1994, a fellow named Barnett Helzberg was walking past the Plaza Hotel in New York City on his way to a meeting when he noticed a woman in a bright red suit calling out: "Warren Buffett! Wait!" He stopped to watch the conversation between the woman, who made it known she was a Berkshire Hathaway shareholder and Warren Buffett fan, and the man widely acknowledged as the most successful investor, *the* Warren Buffett. Buffett was patient and gracious. As it happened, Helzberg was in New York that day to meet with investment bankers about taking his company public or selling it. At the time, his Helzberg Diamonds operated 143 stores nationwide. As the conversation between the woman in the red suit and Buffett ended, Helzberg approached Buffett, introduced himself, and then, rather daringly, told him why he should buy the 79-year-old family jewelry business. The conversation lasted only several minutes. Buffett told Helzberg to send him information and promised it would be looked at and kept confidential. One year later, Buffett purchased Helzberg Diamonds and it joined the Berkshire Hathaway portfolio of companies.

Was this a "lucky" encounter?

I'd say so. But luck had very little to do with the Helzberg family building and developing a successful company that fit Buffett's criteria for achieving far above par financial results compared to competitors, or for having the "stones" to accost Warren Buffett on a street corner and make an elevator pitch out of the blue. Most would so fear rejection they'd never leap on such a lucky encounter at all. They'd later play *woulda, shoulda, coulda* in their mind. Most entrepreneurs do not construct companies of such great value that someone like Buffett, then the second richest man in the world, would want to acquire it. None of that is luck.

Luck is real, good and bad. It can't be denied. But very few if any great business successes or other great achievements can be principally attributed to luck. If and when a stroke of good luck arrives, you have to be thoroughly prepared and have the guts to capitalize on it. Tom Brady, the GOAT, was a sixth-round draft choice warming the bench of the New England Patriots when starting quarterback Drew Bledsoe got injured. Bad luck for Drew, good luck for Tom. It was the opportunity that made the rest of Tom's career and the Tom Brady Story possible. Would Brady have somehow emerged at another time, maybe traded to another team, without this incident? Maybe, maybe not. What we can know is that if Brady had not been ready, mentally and physically, to step up and perform at a high level at any moment he was called on, he might have played poorly, been judged a failure, and never been the GOAT. Also, if and when bad luck occurs, you have to be resilient and resourceful in responding to it, making it just a blip on your story, or even converting it from bad luck to good. Author of the all-time best-selling success book *Think and Grow Rich*, Napoleon Hill, asserted that in EVERY adversity lies the seeds of greater opportunity or benefit. My own life story is a series of adversities converted to opportunities.

Good Luck Is Only an Invitation to Act

Luck is real, good and bad. It can't be denied. But it is almost never luck that rules. Instead, it is what we do about it when it confronts us.

A fine example is my longtime friend and colleague Lee Milteer. Lee grew up in a family that had no money, no role models for success, and no support—her parents both believed she needed to find a husband and settle down, not find a career where she could flourish. No one around her expressed any confidence in her ever accomplishing anything extraordinary. Lee raised herself above it all, to become a best-selling author, a famous and credible professional speaker and trainer, develop a successful coaching business working with entrepreneurs, and a publisher of various courses and programs like "Millionaire Smarts." She built her dream home, a multimillion-dollar beachfront home (and home office) in Virginia Beach.

At the start, Lee had no money for advertising or marketing, so she concentrated on getting what is now called earned media—and she was relentless about it. Zig Ziglar used to tell a story about the saleswoman who was deaf to a "No" yelled into her ear but could hear a whispered "Yes" a mile away. He might as well have been describing Lee Milteer. She researched and called and sent her PR material to every local radio and TV show, ignoring the "not interested" responses and going back to every producer with another idea for having her on as a guest, again and again. On one local cable station, on a real estate show, she was interviewed and noticed by the operators of the station. They offered her a show of her own, with no pay. She took it. Used it to learn how to thrive on TV. She then started reaching out to national and international shows, trying to "ladder up." This led to her invitation to appear on the $1 daytime talk show in Canada, *The Dini Petty Show*, sort of Oprah of Canada.

On the same day she was booked to appear, a famous author and speaker on success subjects, Brian Tracy, was also booked. As the show's time drew near, it became clear that Brian's delayed flight would not arrive in Toronto in time, so Lee was asked to take more time. She had with her a copy of her newest audio program, just arrived at her hotel by Federal Express from the publisher. She carried it onto the set, and in her first appearance of many to come on *The Dini Petty Show*, she used the airtime gained by Brian's non-appearance to show and talk about the program, and provide her office phone number for orders. She delivered a commercial spontaneously, without permission! That day and a few following days, $110,000 of sales occurred—even though she had not prepared for handling the inbound calls and had only her one assistant answering her one line, and for some hours only an answering machine. This event provided needed revenue for growing her business, made her a regular "life advice expert" on *The Dini Petty Show*, impressed her publisher and made her viable as an author, and otherwise poured fuel into her career. Ultimately, Lee has appeared on CBS, NBC, ABC, and FOX as an expert guest and interviewed in every imaginable media from the *Wall Street Journal* to *Glamour*. No college degree. No formal training in PR.

Was she lucky that Brian Tracy was stuck on a delayed flight? Lucky that her publisher FedEx'd her new audio program to her at her hotel? Yes. And my friend and colleague Brian Tracy had the bad luck of a late flight.

But, like my Tom Brady and Barnett Helzberg examples, had Lee not been mentally prepared for an unexpected opportunity, alert for one, creative in response to it, and bold enough to capitalize on it, she might merely have been on the show for extra minutes, answered a few more interview questions, and had it all pass as uneventful.

Throughout her career, Lee has heard and overheard many people remarking on how lucky she has been. Lucky to be on the biggest seminar events with famous business speakers as well as Hollywood celebrities, ignoring the six years of grinding it out, doing small seminars for low pay in 100 cities a year. Lucky to be a multi-book published author, ignoring the rejection slips, the enormous amount of work publicizing and promoting a book so there's reason for a publisher to want another one. Lucky to have landed clients like AT&T, Ford, Disney, FedEx, dozens of other Fortune 1000 companies, ignoring the amount of relentless pursuit of them. Lee says, "I make my own luck."

RESOURCE ALERT!

A free Video Series by Lee Milteer on *The Five Types of Energy: Mental, Emotional, Financial, Physical, and Spiritual* is available at FiveTypesOfEnergy.com. You can also access other Lee Milteer Resources at Milteer.com.

One more example, to hammer home this vital point: my friend and an expert videographer who I rely on, Ron Sheetz, owner of RJ Media Magic.

It didn't seem to be an auspicious opportunity. Shortly after starting his own video production company, a friend referred somebody who wanted to put together a tribute video, mostly of scrapbook photographs, for his father's 60th birthday party. Ron's friend knew he was hungry. Ron took the job. While completing it, he engaged in casual conversation with the client, and found he was the owner of a large mortgage company. (As a side note, it's worth keeping in mind that everybody is more than one thing.) Conversation yielded that business's biggest challenge: recruiting top-producing loan officers. Ron suggested producing a video for loan officer recruiting. That project's success led to Ron being recruited to be Senior Vice President of Marketing, at a six-figure salary (in 2004), where Ron developed the eighth-largest subprime lender, making the Inc. 500 and Entrepreneur 100 lists.

At the same time, Ron continued developing his video production business, as what we now call a side hustle. The limited time mandated very efficient client acquisition. Luckily, the owners of the mortgage company were followers of mine and introduced Ron to my methods. Ron's first exposure to me was at one of my multi-day Super Conferences in 2006. There, Ron alertly caught me say: "Decide who your ideal client is, then focus *all* your efforts on attracting that client, and no efforts on any other clients." Ron went home and analyzed his past and present clients, identifying commonalities of the most valuable ones, and made a target list of certain companies that appeared to match that criteria. He decided that I should be on that list!

Ron became actively involved with everything on what we euphemistically call Planet Dan. He joined the No B.S. Inner Circle, attended every possible event from national conferences to local groups, joined one of our mastermind groups, and made himself visible at every turn. He got business from some of my Members, and in 2010, I had a conversation with him about possibly having him handle the audio/video on-site and the videotaping of one of my upcoming events. The next day, a gigantic, wall poster–size pink "While You Were Out" phone message slip arrived by Federal Express with all his contact information.

It Only Takes One

Ron leveraged what is called a "prestige client" with a significant circle of influence—me. In any business or any career, just one such customer, client, patient, or "name" can make you magnetic.

Since then, Ron has worked on dozens of projects for me and for my clients, from marketing videos starring tennis champion Chris Evert to video advertising for groups of dentists and orthodontists. He has managed the A/V at my mastermind group meetings. Today, he is my go-to guy for everything A/V, including speaking engagements done via Zoom from my home office. He has grown a loyal clientele from my Members and clients worth millions of dollars.

Was his successful "invasion" of Planet Dan, populated by hundreds of the most successful marketing consultants, advisors, and agencies, and of marketing-oriented entrepreneurs ripe with ideal clients for him, a gift of good luck? Yes, there was a lucky moment. I referenced it above. But it might easily have gone by without notice. Ron took it and by his ingenuity and effort and planting himself in a place of fertile opportunity, he made something of it. He did that. Luck didn't.

RESOURCE ALERT!

Ron Sheetz has created a business inside his business: getting great patient testimonials for a dentist on video, and consulting on their best uses. His methods are for dentists and other doctors, but can translate to many other businesses. For a free copy of Ron's book *Your Patient Attraction Secret Weapon: How to Have a Referral-Driven Dental Practice and Never Advertise Again,* text Ron at 216-365-9138. Provide your complete mailing address and email address.

One of the most interesting pieces of my entire career in consulting, writing, speaking, and writing advertising copy and campaigns exists because of a casual, unplanned, off-the-cuff, oh-by-the-way conversation between Bill Guthy and me at the conclusion of a meeting where I sold Bill the manufacturing portion of an audiocassette company I was running at the time. Our meeting had absolutely nothing to do with his other business: TV infomercials. But after concluding all our other business, I asked, purely as a courtesy and curiosity, how his *Think and Grow Rich* infomercial was doing. He said its results were slipping—then, on the spur of the moment, asked if I might look at it and come up with any ideas to bring its performance back up. That turned into a 35-year continuing relationship with the Guthy-Renker Corporation AND many other lucrative opportunities and prominence for me in the infomercial industry.

How can you call that anything but luck?

I can. I call it: being opportunistic.

A very popular quote, "The harder I work, the luckier I get," has merit. I believe in it in principle, because I believe in the work ethic in principle. Through work, you can put yourself in positions where you can get lucky. I think you can learn the art of constantly putting yourself into situations where good luck can occur. You can even give luck a nudge now and then. If I had just completed my deal with Bill Guthy and not expressed curiosity about everything else he was doing, I might never have gotten entrée to the infomercial industry. That's giving good luck a little, helpful nudge.

CONTRARIAN SUCCESS STRATEGY

Good luck exists. Some people are going to get "lucky breaks" whether they deserve them or not, whether you deserved them more than they did, and there's not a thing you can do about all that. It is as random as where raindrops fall. So don't let yourself get eaten up inside with envy or jealousy. Focus, instead, on putting yourself in as many situations and circumstances where good luck can occur for you as possible. Then you'll get your share.

Bad luck exists, and bad luck happens to good people. It doesn't have to have permanent effects. The "magic trick" of successful people is creatively converting adversities into opportunities. Being resilient and resourceful turns bad luck into good luck.

In both cases, good and bad luck, the determinant of success is what YOU do with it.

CHAPTER 9

Warning: You Can't Get Rich Quick. Can You?

Tom Seaver: "What time is it?"
Yogi Berra: "You mean now?"

If haste makes waste, you can't prove it by John Elway of the Denver Broncos, one of the greatest artists of the two-minute drill ever. If there were two minutes left in the game, you'd better be beating Denver by more than two touchdowns. That darned Elway could suffer through an entire game of throwing badly timed passes, getting sacked, running desperately to escape the rush, receivers dropping passes, and sluggish efforts from his backs, then suddenly light up the field and elevate everybody's play and beat you by packing more offense into the last two minutes than occurred in the previous fifty-eight. Cleveland Browns fan know this all too well. We know it as "The Drive." Since Elway, quite a few quarterbacks have demonstrated mastery of the two-minute drill. Brady was famous for it just before halftime and again at the end of games. How can you waste most of a game, then, with extreme haste, still win?

Is this "two-minute drill" phenomenon unique to football? Or even to sports? Not at all.

There are any number of people I know in business who work best and deliver their best work when under enormous time pressure. My friend Gary Halbert was, arguably, one of the smartest, most successful direct marketing copywriters in the world. But, like the famous fictitious detective Nero Wolfe, who would only work when prodded by a dwindling bank account, his aide-de-camp Archie Goodwin, and extraordinary circumstances (like a corpse arriving on his doorstep or someone machine-gunning all the orchids in his rooftop greenhouse), Gary only rose out of lethargy to do brilliant work in very, very short spurts, only when his own dwindling finances made it absolutely essential, and then only when intrigued by a project and nagged by staff and client alike. He was legendary for both his extraordinary talent and his reluctance to employ it. I have known him to sit on a project for weeks, dodging, stalling, finding every imaginable excuse to set the work aside for one more day. Finally, though, with no escape route left, with only hours left to deliver on a promise, he would accomplish in minutes what would take most pros in his field weeks to do. After being stalled by Gary for weeks, one extremely frustrated client flew to Key West, to camp out with Gary and make him write his ad. After three days of running errands, dining out, and roaming around with still no ad, the defeated client was getting dropped off at the airport when Gary got two old brown bags off the floor of his car and hastily wrote the ad with a marker, working on the hood of his car. The ad made hundreds of thousands of dollars.

I tell people, I am the hardest working lazy person on the planet. If there is not an almost insurmountable pile of work confronting me, pressing deadlines prodding me, and plenty of pressure to perform driving me, I won't get anything done at all. And I can do more quality work in an hour than most people do in a week. I think I could run that two-minute offense.

There Is Only One Speed: Faster

I am old enough to recall when Federal Express's next-day delivery was an amazing breakthrough that changed everything. Today, we are accustomed to and demanding of: INSTANT.

In business, speed to market is now vital. You don't have to be first or fastest but you can't be fourth and slow either. With every idea, product, service, start-up, ad campaign—the race is on.

No one can rest either. Steve Jobs said that if you are succeeding or leading you have to remember there are two kids in a garage staying up all night working on the idea they'll use to take everything away from you. It's a lot truer now than when he said it.

Slow 'n steady rarely wins now.

Maybe it never did.

High Achievers and "Rushing Sickness"

If you want to insist that "haste makes waste," you'll be forced to acknowledge that high achievers accept or ignore the waste and make haste anyway. In the book *Profiles of Power and Success*, Dr. Landrum notes that the super-achievers studied were all afflicted with a kind of "rushing sickness": They ate, talked, drove, even slept fast. Napoleon graduated from college in half the normal time. Walt Disney went on prolonged, fast-paced working binges broken up by periods of complete collapse, and slept on the couch at his office nearly half his adult life because he resented the time wasted commuting. At age 19, Picasso was turning out a new painting each day. He was warned by art dealers that he would ruin the market for his work. (They were wrong.)

Impatience and intolerance for anything impeding their progress characterized every super successful man and woman featured in this extraordinary book, which I recommend highly. As I think about it, the most successful people I've ever worked with—and there have been plenty of them—have exhibited both of these characteristics in great abundance.

Those who are constantly harping at you to slow down and take it easy probably do not understand what makes you tick, what gives you fulfillment in life, or what is necessary to succeed in the environment you operate in. While those with "the rushing sickness" do admittedly pay a price for their achievements, this is also their key to high achievement. Further, success-oriented urgency does not necessarily have to create waste or require sacrifice of quality. Most people work slower than need be.

Well, What About This "You Can't Get Rich Quick" Rule?

All your life, you've been warned against so-called get-rich-quick schemes and against the entire idea of getting rich quick. Had a finger wagged in your face while being lectured about patience, "paying your dues," climbing ladders.

What if those warnings have been getting in your way? What if everything you've been told about speed has come from slow people? And is wrong?

In one of the Renegade Millionaire Mastermind Groups at NO BS / MAGNETIC MARKETING, we have a young man from Malaysia, who took his small $3 million company to $35 million *in one year*. He says that his commitment to high speed and mega-growth created its own kind of momentum and magnetic attraction. This has been my experience with countless clients over many years. What my friend Jim Rohn called the secret of MASSIVE action attracts people, capital, media attention, and excited customers like nothing else. When you are doing big things *fast*, the world notices.

THE PHENOMENON®

There is something I call THE PHENOMENON®, a time in your career and life when—suddenly—you achieve more in 10 months than you did in the previous 10 years. This happens organically to a lot of people, once, maybe twice. Some take advantage of it, others don't. It can, however, be deliberately triggered. There are known Triggers of it. What was slow, methodical, struggling progress can suddenly go to warp speed, by use of one or several of these Triggers.

My clients Preston Schmidli and McBilly Sy are good poster boys for THE PHENOMENON®. Their company, Good Vibe Squad, is not a metaphysical group as its name might suggest. It is a direct-to-consumer lead generation and advertising agency for residential mortgage originators, brokers, and loan officers. When Preston and McBilly started it, in 2017, they were each rebounding from prior business and personal tragedies, and financed this start-up quite literally with blood money; Preston gave two liters of blood a week to a plasma center. McBilly was working two dead-end jobs, one at a blood bank. In 2018, the business barely crawled above the $100,000 mark, growing at a tortoise's pace. A pace that would have them starve out before ever succeeding.

They met through the ClickFunnels Community created by Russell Brunson, who wrote this book's Foreword. Through it, they were also introduced to me. Proving two heads are better than one, they hit on a PHENOMENON® Trigger: direct outreach and offer to a curated list, driving to a telephone sales appointment positioned as a free consultation. No "cold" telephone or in-person prospecting. Marketing used to get a qualified prospect *to ask for a sales presentation.* This elegantly simple plan is used by a number of my most successful clients, including a business coaching company serving small law firms, a real estate investing group serving only dentists three to seven years from retirement, a specialty medical clinic, and a dozen others. Preston and McBilly hand-assembled 4,800 agents by viewing their websites and judging them good prospects. They then wrote a one-page ad for their service with the offer of the free tele-consult call, emailed the 4,800 targets inviting them to the ad online, and held their breath.

In 2019, their revenue leaped to $630,000. In 2021, $1.7 million. In 2022, $3 million. As I write this, they are on pace to break $5 million. The big leap that provided all the upward momentum was from 2018 to 2019, from the one Trigger they uncovered and adapted. Can ONE discovery change everything? Yes. Russell Brunson says, "You are only ONE funnel away from your fortune."

"The COMMON advice that we got in the slow years that we got from just about everybody was that we just needed to work harder," Preston says, "and that is the same bad advice given by sales managers and others to struggling loan officers—who we rescue! Nothing wrong with hard work, but on what? If it is applied to a faulty plan, you get calluses. You have to be determined to find or cobble together a more effective plan if yours or one sold to you by others is not rewarding your hard work."

They are aiming at $15 million with another PHENOMENON® Trigger: multiplication by heavy reinvestment in fuel for a proven machine with room to run. (Read that Trigger most carefully!) McBilly says, "You have to be willing to sacrifice personally in the short term, to reinvest in your business, to fuel another surge of speed of growth. We see a lot of friends in business stall and tread water in place then drift backward because they won't take this kind of risk or make this sacrifice."

RESOURCE ALERT!

You can see some of the powerful resources that Preston and McBilly have created for the home mortgage industry at goodvibesquad.com/free-resources.

Then there's my friend, client, and business colleague Russell Brunson, who provided Preston and McBilly an environment outside of the mortgage industry, where different success models could be seen. Outwitting two highly funded, venture capital–backed competitors, Russell took his start-up, ClickFunnels, from zero to $100 million in just 36 months, with its only financing from his one credit card. As his PHENOMENON® Trigger, he assembled a multi-tactic system for mitigating customer acquisition cost. His competitors had but one, and many entrepreneurs make the mistake of "just one thing at a time" when their chance at speed lies in synergistic multiplicity. To be fair, he had years of "slow" before this PHENOMENON® experience. He had false starts and went down blind alleys. He was also a fierce seeker and acquirer of how to succeed information. He began studying me when he was still in high school and in his first fledgling business. He joined my company's mastermind group just in advance of his 36-month sprint. He now has a family of companies under the ClickFunnels umbrella, including the company and membership organization I originally created, No B.S. Inner Circle. As I write this, he's on his way at a brisk pace to $200 million. All ignited by one Trigger: a multiplicity of offsets to new customer acquisition cost, not just the industry norm of one.

Turn on Media, Turn Your Money Machine to "High Speed"

Years ago, my friend Robert Ringer propelled his controversial book *Winning Through Intimidation* to national best-seller status, and into a national conversation that made him famous, by not relying on traditional book publishers or their practices. Instead, he self-published long before that got in vogue as it is now, long before Amazon existed. He then bought full-page, copy-loaded ads in major newspapers for his book. In his great book, he talks about having a "Leap-Frog Strategy." Climbing ladders organized by others is slow. Leap-frogging can be fast.

Media can give you THE PHENOMENON®. Could be mastering TikTok, Facebook, Google, Amazon, or other online media. Could be good, solid legacy media like radio, TV, or print. Even still, a newspaper ad campaign.

Don't tell Bill Guthy and Greg Renker that you can't get rich quick. In 1987, Bill Guthy, then 33, running an audiocassette duplicating company mostly serving speakers and seminar companies, and his golfing buddy, Greg Renker, then 31, talked about the enormous volume of cassettes Bill's company was duping for a guy teaching get-rich-in-real-estate seminars via a cable TV "infomercial," a new form of paid advertising. Deciding to jump in and sell something they both believed in, they scraped together, borrowed, and begged for $100,000, secured the rights to sell an audiocassette package based on Napoleon Hill's classic book *Think and Grow Rich,* and produced the first "docu-mercial," hosted by all-time great NFL quarterback Fran Tarkenton. By 1988, that show had grossed $10 million, a big number at that time. I was fortunate to get involved then in consulting, writing, and producing for Greg and Bill, helped with sales-boosting revisions to this first show, and I continued to consult with them as they built a $200-million-a-year business in less than 10 years. Their Trigger for all this was bringing celebrity hosts to infomercials. But there was another Trigger that created a second, bigger PHENOMENON®: their switch from shows selling intellectual property products bought once to shows selling skincare and cosmetic products that got used up and reordered again and again by the same customer. This facilitated putting customers into continuity, auto-shipping a supply every month, auto-charging a credit card every month. The biggest star in that portfolio was PROACTIV®, made the #1 selling home acne treatment in America, by TV infomercials hosted by a number of celebrities. They sold that part of their company for around $1 BILLION to Nestle. As I write this, they have another hit product, a wrinkle remover, Crepe Erase. Their formula for success, which evolved slowly starting in the late 1980s, has proved reliable and repeatable, its own PHENOMENON®.

In some respects, Greg and Bill have had no choice but to keep "getting rich quick" over and over again and helping others do the same. The infomercial industry is very "hit driven," not unlike the entertainment industry. Trends are important. Predicting consumers' next burning desire is at the core of the business. And having the economic muscle and guts to massively roll out a successful infomercial and its product fast is necessary, because a number of knockoffs quickly follow every success. A new infomercial can go from idea to completed show on the air, selling products, in as quickly as three to six weeks. In the infomercial industry, "quick" is the norm.

Bill and Greg are not alone. Home shopping channels like QVC and HSN have the awesome power of creating overnight millionaires. I personally know of several people who have gone on one of these channels with their product for the very first time and, in one weekend, gone from nowhere to $250,000, $500,000, or more in sales plus larger, instant commitments for future purchases from the network. Little-known products, like an obscure citrus oil–based spot remover, become household name brands almost instantly thanks to this unique exposure.

One of My Own PHENOMENON®
Stories & the Power of OPC

There are three kinds of "fuel" for a business: OPM, OPR, and OPC. Most entrepreneurs lust and chase after OPM—Other People's Money—but this carries costly price tags like giving up big chunks of equity in your company, taking on opinionated partners, taking on high interest debt, and otherwise sacrificing *permanently*. This is sometimes necessary or advisable, but there are other types of alternative capital. One is OPR: Other People's Resources. For example, if somebody has a sales platform—like Amazon—you can rent space in it and benefit from its traffic. If somebody has a factory or a telemarketing center or a printing company with unused capacity, you can wheel 'n deal to use it to produce what you need. Something as simple as outsourcing the handling of inbound calls versus having a full-time employee and house fixed costs is use of OPR.

My favorite is OPC: Other People's Customers. I helped a client launch a franchise for doctors at an unheard-of selling speed in the industry by persuading someone with a good number of qualified doctors as his clients to cooperate. They were brought together by him, for a presentation by my client, and we accomplished more in a few hours than most new franchisors could do in many months.

One of my personal experiences with this was as a professional speaker. I was successful at it, but modestly so, and mostly absent any real fame or celebrity. I labored in oblivion. Keep in mind, I was always speaking not just for the day's income, but primarily to acquire customers who would stay, buy products and services repeatedly, become my "members," and refer. Speaking "small," to audiences of dozens to hundreds at a time, keeping a dozen or a few dozen in ongoing relationships, was slow going. In the year prior to my PHENOMENON® Breakthrough, I managed to round up about 1,000 customers.

Then came the opportunity. A new client, Peter Lowe, sought me out, to consult on ways to boost revenue of his public success seminars. One of the strategies I proposed was adding an unadvertised bonus speaker at the very end of the day, a surprise to the audience, an unknown person who, if advertised, would not pull audience, but who could sell info-resources successfully in that bad time slot, under those adverse conditions. (The speaker and his company split sales revenue 50/50.) He wanted to test the idea, and we agreed that I'd be the guinea pig. I had a suitable info-product that I sold from the stage. I appointed myself to the new position I had created.

The SUCCESS events were fast growing, quickly full days in 25 to 27 cities a year, in basketball arenas, with 15,000 to 25,000 attendees, brought from about a $1 million ad budget per city. Virtually all those attracted to these events were perfect customers for me. And I was there, every time, for nine consecutive years. The audiences shrank throughout the day, so I often had only 2,000 or 3,000 staying to hear me. But still I would sell to 300 or so in every city, over 7,000 in a year; because of their quality, over 2,000 converted to ongoing customers/members. I was— for free—acquiring Peter's best customers that cost him over $20 million a year to get. That was good, but there was a bigger benefit: Being on these events with audiences of this size, events covered by media, along with former U.S. presidents, Hollywood celebrities, legendary entrepreneurs, as well as the top business and motivational speakers of the day like Zig Ziglar, made me a celebrity by association. It poured gasoline on everything. This lifted me as a book author, speaker at other events, and gave me a lot of access into many OPC "nests" I would not have gotten without this celebrity. I estimate its overall OPC effect was about 1,000 new "sticky" customers/members a month vs. the old pace of 1,000 a year. That's a 12X, for those weak in math.

In many cases, OPC beats OPM, hands down.

Why "Slow" Is So Much Harder Than "Fast"

If you'll examine the source of all the warnings you've had against the idea of getting rich quick, you will find that most, if not all, have come to you from well-intentioned people who have not gotten rich at all, at any pace. It is considerably easier to be a sage expert in what not to do than in how to do something. All these warnings must be taken with not a grain but a whole shaker full of salt.

Just about any rich person will tell you that slow is harder than fast, because it is almost impossible to create momentum while moving slowly. A two-by-four across the tracks will bring a however-many-ton locomotive just starting to move to a grinding halt, while a train moving at full speed will turn that same board into toothpicks and the passengers probably won't even feel the bump. If possible, you want momentum on your side.

CONTRARIAN SUCCESS STRATEGY

Why not get rich quick? There's no good reason—only past negative conditioning—prohibiting you from taking a quantum leap, from triggering THE PHENOMENON®. Slow 'n steady does not win every race. Different strategies are best for different opportunities, and often, speed and being quick is the only way you will get rich with a particular opportunity.

If you would like more information, free, about PHENOMENON® TRIGGERS, you can visit MagneticMarketing.com/phenomenon.

CHAPTER 10

When a Dog Bites You, Do You Have to Say, "Thank You, Nice Doggie"?

"To avoid criticism, do nothing, say nothing, be nothing."

—*Elbert Hubbard*

D r. Maxwell Maltz, creator of Psycho-Cybernetics, with whom I co-authored *The New Psycho-Cybernetics*, identified Immunity to Criticism as a key characteristic of highly successful people. He likened this emotional immune system and mental health to your physical immune system and overall health. Most people live and try to conduct business while in deathly fear of criticism and others' disapproval. Many conflate avoiding criticism with being polite, but, in reality, it forces being subservient. Is this the path to success, in a crowded, cluttered, anti-differentiation marketplace?

If you saw the famous "Soup Nazi" episode of Seinfeld, you saw a true antihero of customer service at work. He was only a slight exaggeration from the true, "classic" New York deli owner who freely yells at customers, takes crap from no one, and would rather lose a customer than an argument any day of the week. Here, in my neighborhood, we have a big business jammed into a small space, Stan's Bakery. It is run by a small, tough Polish lady who has plastered the place with signs warning customers about bad behavior. One by the cakes says: "If you call more than once to check on your cake being ready on time, there's a $5 charge." On the glass door of the freezer case: "Don't open these doors to look. They're glass. You can look through them." Insulting? Offensive? Or the stuff of legend? Her daughter has won awards for cake design, and won a reality show competition. The little bakery is famous far and wide less for the awards and more for the owner's "soup Nazi-ish" personality. Customers offended (and lacking a sense of humor) come in once and never again, and that is just fine with this owner because good, well-behaved customers (with a sense of humor) love her and the place and not only frequently patronize it, but act as evangelists telling friends "you've *got to* see this bakery."

Since the China Virus and the aftereffects of extreme employee shortages causing reduced hours, long waits, and overall, poor customer service, business owners striving to let the customer always be right are struggling mightily. Whether it is fulfilled or not, it is certainly true that the axiom "The customer is always right" is as American as the flag. We teach it and preach it and write one book after another about how to achieve it. It is a highly promoted rule. And, like most highly promoted rules, it's a bad one.

If you have ever worked in retail or in a service business, you have had "The customer is always right" drummed into your head as the ultimate gospel. This means that no matter how unreasonable or irrational the customer, you must chomp down on your tongue, never argue, and strive to accommodate and pacify.

Herb Kelleher, a founder of Southwest Airlines, does not agree, and I don't either. "I think one of the biggest betrayals of employees a boss can possibly commit is insisting that the customer is always right," Herb said. "The customer is frequently wrong. In those cases, we have to support our employees. And we try not to cater to those kinds of customers. We write to them and say, 'Fly somebody else. Don't abuse our people.'"

Obviously, we want satisfied, happy customers who'll stay, pay, and refer—but not at the expense of accepting every imaginable bad behavior.

You can have well-behaved customers if you will be selective about who you attract and you clearly explain what is expected of them.

There Are Some Customers You Are Better Off Without

You do NOT want all the customers you can get. To many, that's a heretical statement. The idea many business owners have is to get every customer they possibly can and do everything they can to keep them. My own philosophy is quite different.

First of all, I "fire" customers and clients from time to time when it seems advisable. For example, in our publications and mail-order business I ran for 20 years or so, we guaranteed customers' satisfaction unconditionally, no questions asked, no strings attached, no hassle, and we meant it. However, when someone returned one product for a refund, bought another, and returned it for a refund, we surmised two things: One, we were unlikely to satisfy this customer in the future, and, two, it was highly probable that this person was ripping us off by copying our product. Because of the high costs of handling returns and refunds, such a customer had no value to us. They were a liability, not an asset. We "blacklisted" them. We removed them from all of our mailing lists, and if they ordered via some other stimulus, such as a magazine ad, their name was "flagged" and we refused their order. I no longer personally run that business, but the policy stands.

Second, just like Herb Kelleher, I believe you have to back up your own team members when they are right—so I occasionally had to write a customer a letter chastising them and terminating them as a customer. Certainly there are times when our staff or I were "wrong." We fumbled the ball. And in those cases, we owed customers apologies and every reasonable effort to make up for the gaffe. But some customers are simply too demanding or difficult to be worth having.

With 50 years of this behind me, I can assure you that the practice built an exceptionally valuable company. When it was sold, it commanded an above-par, way above "formula" price largely because of the demonstrable quality of our customers and the demonstrable absence of bad ones. Clients who followed my lead on this also built not just profitable companies but exceptionally valuable ones. Bean counters don't know how to value this, but savvy entrepreneurs do.

Only you can decide to what extent you want to go to satisfy even extraordinarily difficult customers. But buying into "The customer is always right" idea wholesale, without caveat, just doesn't make sense.

A Customer for Every Business, a Business for Every Customer

My private client Michael Huang is a great example of intentionally acquiring the right customers so those customers can be right.

Michael operates a large, growing, thriving martial arts business. He says, "At the U.S. Kuo Shu Academy, we have a strict policy of accepting only new students who have undergone a physical and mindset evaluation, and their parent or parents have also been interviewed. Then a trial lesson is required. And yes, we do turn some students away. We know the *exact* kind of person we are looking for, and we are more concerned with that than we are with simple quantity. We are not just making a sale or engaging in transactions, like a Walmart. I think of us more like Apple, getting committed customers for life. If our goal for a school is $1 million a year, I keep in mind that Apple needs only about 1,000 customers to hit that mark but Walmart needs as many as 100,000. We present and deliver a premium quality product and we need to charge premium fees to support it. There is a 'type' of parent and young person who will appreciate and respect that and there are customers who won't. They might still enroll if I have a salesperson who can sell ice to Eskimos, but those customers would very likely be disruptive to our culture, difficult to manage, unsuccessful, and possibly generate bad word of mouth. We want to *prevent* that."

Michael is the author of several books, including *Building Habits, Self-Discipline and Character Through Martial Arts,* that are required reading for students and parents. "We have a formal Code of Conduct," Michael says, "that is explained to each student when they begin, and that *is* enforced. Dan Kennedy says: Customers *can* be trained. He also says that most business owners are cowards about this. Early on, I had some timidity about it, fearing loss of needed customers. But I have learned through experience that the key to the customer always feeling they are right and getting excellent treatment is to carefully screen and select the right customers and to teach them our business's purpose, values, and culture. I think any business can do the same."

From age 3, Michael Huang has been refining his Kung Fu martial arts skills, learning from his father, Grandmaster Huang Chen-Liang, who immigrated to America in 1973, and is known throughout the world as a martial arts thought-leader. Michael also developed business skills, starting with a stint at a major investment banking firm after college, and studying the disciplines of advertising, marketing, selling, and managing a business by finding mentors, taking courses, and reading countless books by and about successful entrepreneurs. He has not only

brought all this to his school, but as a coach to hundreds of other school owners throughout the U.S. and abroad. He leads an international association of Kuo Shu academies.

RESOURCE ALERT!

You can find out more about Michael Huang and about his businesses and books at USKuoShu.com.

Michael is a testament to the idea, strange to so many, that organizing an entire business, from its advertising messages through its operations, to attract precisely the right customer is a far, far more certain path to success than is bending over backwards to apply "the customer is always right" to the wrong customers!

One of the key strategies I teach in my "Magnetic Marketing" speeches, seminars, and systems is, rather than advertising your product, service, or business, advertise FOR the customers or clients you want. The sooner you determine who your "perfect match customer" is and target that person AND deliberately repel those who do not fit that description, the better.

Not only isn't the customer always right, but every customer isn't always right for your business.

CONTRARIAN SUCCESS STRATEGY

The customer is not always right. Of course, you should exert reasonable effort to understand a customer's dissatisfaction, respond positively if possible, accommodate if you can, and preserve a valuable relationship if possible. But you also have an obligation to support yourself or your team members when they are right. Also, strategically targeting customers most likely to be satisfied by your combination of products, services, capabilities, and style of doing business, and periodically purging your customer base of those who are not well matched with you, so as to add more who are, will lead to the most profitable business, most productive staff, happiest customers, and greatest peace of mind. In Chapter 5, Craig Proctor said he had achieved what looked like success and was financial success, but was still failure in disguise. One sure way to wind up with success that is failure in disguise is dependency on ill-suited customers you dislike and can't satisfy.

CHAPTER 11

"It Takes Money to Make Money"

"I was the ultimate double threat: broke and inexperienced."

—*Hugh Hefner, discussing his start-up of* Playboy *magazine*

I suspect more people give up on their entrepreneurial dreams and ideas because of lack of money than any other reason. *I don't have the money to do it. I don't know anybody who does. I can't get the money.* Nuts.

There ARE plenty of experts who will run you through the conventional build-a-business-plan process, forecast two to five years without profit, budget for all manner of equipment and overhead, and calculate that you need somewhere between a zillion and two zillion dollars to start your business. Yet the ranks of entrepreneur-millionaires are chock-full of people who ignored all that, started with next to no money, and somehow clawed and finagled their way to the top. In fact, it is often more harmful than helpful to be sufficiently capitalized and not to have to struggle for survival. Resourcefulness is more powerful than resources.

I have long taught: If you can't make money without money, you won't make money with money either. And if you're going to back somebody, pick an entrepreneur who has proven he can survive without adequate capital.

It's easy to forget that Walt and Roy Disney were broke when they opened Disneyland, Apple was started by two punks in a garage, and Bezos packed boxes of books and schlepped them to the post office himself. These days, the lure of seed capital and multiple rounds of financing from Wall Street or Silicon Valley is enormously seductive. People prefer getting started with a lot of money, but not only isn't that always possible, it's not necessarily best.

In Chapter 9, I cited three types of capital in addition to your own: OPM, OPR, and OPC. Other People's Money. Other People's Resources. Other People's Customers.

The first comes with big, fat price tags. Sacrifice of equity and of control. Founders are even forced out of the companies they started as a cost of OPM—frequently. Often deals made to get OPM have to be expensively reversed later. Walt and Roy sold exclusive concessions to companies like Kodak® and sponsorships of individual attractions to automakers, appliance companies, and others under deal-with-the-Devil terms they had to later buy their way out of. (Walt also made a good deal to get desperately needed money for the park by agreeing to give ABC an exclusive weekly TV show. It not only provided cash but acted as a free advertisement for Disney every week.)

The biggest problem with OPM is that it encourages waste, misplaced priorities, and complacency. The end result of this is the same as Margaret Thatcher said about socialism: "Sooner or later you run out of other people's money."

OPR can substitute for capital via renting, borrowing, or barter without sacrifice of equity and without piling up debt.

Always most interesting to me is OPC, Other People's Customers, as I discussed earlier in the book.

If you watch *Shark Tank* alertly, you'll notice different sharks get interested when a business being pitched syncs with the customers of another business they are already invested in. Kevin O'Leary is particularly adept at this, and he told me that he has invested in businesses that probably could not make it without the customers transferable from another company he was already invested in.

The point is: Money isn't everything!. There are a lot of ingenious, inventive substitutes for it that work just as well or, sometimes, better.

How Ignoring Conventional Wisdom About Costs Created a Record-Breaking Infomercial Success

In 1989, the "buzz" in the infomercial industry was that the ante for quality production was up and up and up, and you could no longer put a successful show in the can for less than $200,000 or so. It was also the buzz that a solo, small entrepreneur couldn't get access to enough good media time to make it worthwhile even doing an infomercial. In other words, the rule was: either do business with one of the handful of "big boys" or don't do business at all. In the face of this, I produced a show for my client U.S. Gold for under $30,000. The company's owner, Len Shykind, made his first tentative, timid, doubtful media buy for a whopping $400. Seeing success, he bootstrapped the income to buy more time. Eight years later, he bought his own time direct from the TV stations and cable networks. And his little, "ugly," cheap show put millions of dollars in his pocket and more than tripled the value of his company. This infomercial holds the record as THE longest-running lead generation infomercial in the business opportunity category. And, incidentally, back at its inception, Len started this multimillion-dollar company with less than $1,000.

To be fair, you could not pull that exact low-budget infomercial trick off today. At least I don't think you could. But in inflation-adjusted, proportionate dollars, you probably could. There are also more media opportunities to present products on the screen than there were in 1989, like YouTube.

People will always tell you that "you can't afford it." Just be careful about telling yourself that.

Lack of Money Is Just an Excuse

In my book *How to Make Millions with Your Ideas*, I described how Terry Loebel launched Valpak with just $500 in his garage. Nolan Bushnell, who co-founded Atari, the electronic game company forerunner of today's giant computer game industry, with $500 and sold it to Warner four years later for $28 million, said that success boils down to just one critical action step: "getting off your ass and doing something."

As I have studied and in many cases met people like Loebel and Bushnell, who have started businesses with nominal sums of money and built giant corporations as well as personal fortunes, I have become thoroughly convinced that lack of money is just an excuse—and all the sage, expert advice about making certain your business is adequately capitalized is a bunch of hooey.

As a result of my book *How to Make Millions with Your Ideas*, I did a lot of talk radio shows and took a lot of calls from people with new product ideas. Over half were whining about how they didn't have enough money to get going and needed somebody to invest in their idea or take it, make it happen, and pay them a royalty. The news to be broken to them was never well received. The truth is that ideas, and people with ideas, are a dime a dozen. People with ideas but not enough guts to do anything with them are a dime a thousand. Sure, licensing deals happen. Sure, people invent widgets, license them to some big company, and become millionaires from royalties alone. People win the lottery, too. But if you want the odds on your side, you'll get off your butt and go to work turning your idea into a business.

Like Ed Lowe did. Ed didn't just start a business; he created the entire "cat litter" industry. He literally stumbled on the idea for gravel-based, absorbent cat box litter in 1947 and, before selling out, built an $85-million-a-year business in a $250-million-a-year industry. His first product was a five-pound paper bag of the gravel. Its label was his handwriting on the bag with a black grease pencil: "Kitty Litter. Takes the Place of Sand. Absorbs and Deodorizes. Ask Kitty. She Knows."

Lowe got his initial retail distribution by loading up his Chevy with bags, driving around from pet shop to pet shop, doing a little demonstration, and getting each store owner to take a few sacks. He spent several years, as he puts it, "out where the rubber meets the road," securing his distribution one store at a time. He literally cornered the market single-handedly. Largely thanks to Ed, the house cat became America's favorite pet, dethroning the dog from that position. *People* magazine said, "In the history of cats, there are two dates of significance: 1500 B.C., when the little creatures were first given shelter inside Egyptian homes, and 1947, when they finally became proper house guests. That was the year Edward Lowe chanced upon the cat world sensation he called Kitty Litter."

You might argue that such a thing cannot be done today. You'd be wrong. Certainly, you might choose to use a more efficient process than driving from store to store all across the country. But nevertheless, you can start a new product or a new brand from scratch, with virtually no capital and no advertising budget, and make it happen.

Technology Makes It Easier Than Ever to Start Businesses with Very Little Money

The barriers to entry have fallen. Countless successful companies start via Facebook, Instagram, TikTok, YouTube, Amazon stores, eBay, Etsy. Companies like GoDaddy make one-stop shop setup of your first online shop easy. Companies like ClickFunnels template the online bridges from advertising and publicity to marketing to selling. Of course, most businesses that start and initially succeed online later move offline as well, but something very big can start small.

I have a client right now who started a new online business fueled only by free SEO (Search Engine Optimization), YouTube videos made from home, and webinars conducted from home. It did $2.3 million its first 12 months, is on pace to double that during its second year, and already has people interested in acquiring it for $8 million. There is NOTHING he's done that anybody couldn't do, beginning with almost no money.

CONTRARIAN SUCCESS STRATEGY

Stop letting lack of money imprison you. There's abundant evidence all around you that you can turn your ideas into a successful enterprise without having a lot of capital. Access to plenty of money will not "make" a business. Having to fight its way into existence without money will not "kill" a really viable business.

CHAPTER 12

Special Contrarian Advice for Young People— and Useful to Others

*"Whatever the majority of people is doing,
under any given circumstance, if you do the exact opposite,
you will probably never make another mistake as long as you live."*

—Earl Nightingale

O ne of the things I hear a lot from recent college grads is the extraordinary difficulty of finding a job in the field they've chosen and prepared for. But I happen to believe that you can get a very beneficial starting-point job, in any field you wish, in just about any company you choose, from the owner, CEO, or other "top dog" of your choice. Here, exactly, is why and how.

First, forget everything you believe or have been told about what you are entitled to. Entitlement Thinking about anything produces failure and frustration. If out of high school or college or changing fields, you are new and unproven, you are entitled to nothing but opportunity.

Second, forget everything you've been told about resumes, your college's placement office, executive placement firms, online job sites, and standard interviewing skills. Just being one of this year's herd sending out resumes and plodding along the traditional normal path is NOT going to get you *abnormal* results. If you want to make something dramatic happen fast, you need a contrarian approach.

How I Got My First Job—Even Though I Was Woefully Unqualified

In 1973, as a high school (only) grad, I needed to get to work and I had decided I wanted to start out in "professional selling." I envisioned a nice, new company car (probably because I was driving a $25 clunker), a salary, commissions, and bonuses, suit-and-tie work, and some glamorous travel. I spotted an ad in the *Cleveland Plain Dealer*: The national sales manager for a publishing company was in town for two days only to hire a sales rep to call on all the bookstores, department stores, and other retailers in a five-state area. For me, "publishing" was a magic word because I had ideas of being a writer and a publisher in the future. And the ad said there was a starting salary of $1,600 to $2,000 a month, commissions, bonuses, expenses, and a company car. It was perfect for me. Unfortunately, I wasn't perfect for it. When I went to the interview, the national sales manager politely explained to me that I was NOT what he was looking for at all. First, I was too young. Second, I had no experience. Third, I didn't have a college education. This position would typically be filled by a 35- to 45-year-old man or woman with a college degree and a significant amount of professional selling experience, not some "kid" right out of high school. And he had several such applicants to choose from. I did my best to sell myself, but he was adamant. I just wasn't qualified.

That's when I pulled the rabbit out of the hat. I said, "Look, you haven't had a rep working this area for six months. Going another three months isn't going to kill you. So here's what I suggest you do: Let me work for you for three months for expenses only, no salary, and I'll drive my own car. If, during those three months, I prove myself to you, you hire me for another three months at half salary but full commissions and bonuses and you furnish the car. If during those three months I prove myself, then you hire me on the regular basis, with full pay and benefits. I'll earn the job."

I knew I wasn't qualified. I certainly wasn't entitled to have it. I did not let that fact interfere.

And I was hired. I immediately had some problems, too. I had to go work the company's booth at the Chicago Gift Show but I didn't have a credit card or enough cash to make the trip. The car I had would never make it running around over five states, and the most money I had to replace it with was $300. But I was hired.

In short order, without company approval, I sort of reinvented the entire selling process and I achieved some records: biggest turnaround of a troubled territory in company history; more full rack placements to new accounts in a quarter than any other rep; new major non-bookstore chain accounts; and more. At the end of three months, I was given my car, full salary, full commissions, and bonuses. I stayed with this company for about a year and a half before switching to self-employment.

A Bold, Challenging Statement Gets This Unqualified Guy the Job That Would Make Him Rich

Another story: Bob Edmiston was young, poorly educated, but determined to get ahead in a career in finance. He worked for a bank, for Chrysler, for Ford, but couldn't get moving. He applied for the position of controller with the upstart Jensen automobile company and was rejected. Not well enough educated. Not enough experience. And so on. But a few months later, the owner called, said he didn't like the guy who had been hired, and invited Bob in for an interview. At the end, the owner said, "You're only 27 years old and that's too young to be a controller and you've never done this kind of a job before. Why should I trust you with all this responsibility?"

Bob answered, "I've read that you started making yourself into a millionaire when you were just 28 years old. I'd like a go at it, too."

This is exactly the kind of gutsy, straightforward approach that entrepreneurs like and respond to. Any other applicant would have squirmed in his seat, trotted out more information about his past jobs, and struggled to justify himself in the face of such a tough question. And most job applicants are concerned with their starting wage, vacation days, and health care—not becoming a millionaire. By not responding like a typical job applicant in any way, shape, or form, Bob hit the mark. He reminded the entrepreneur interviewing him of his own early struggles and desires. This entrepreneur hired Bob on the spot.

As an aside, Bot Edmiston points out that it's never really the length of experience that counts—it's the intensity. "You can work 50 years filing papers and learn nothing," Bob says, "or you can work six months in an intense situation and learn a tremendous amount." Bob had such an intense experience at Jensen. As you may recall, the high-priced luxury sports car was a bust. The company went bankrupt in just nine months with Bob Edmiston as its chief financial controller.

After the bankruptcy, Bob formed a little company called Jensen Parts and Service, with less than $6,000 of capital. In 17 years, Bob built that business up to a value of nearly $450 million.

How I Hired a Protégé for the Wage of $0 a Year

Years ago, a young lady just graduated from Cornell sent me a long, 12-page letter. She explained that she and her parents had been in an audience in Rochester, New York, and seen me speak, that they had all been enormously impressed, that she wanted to learn about direct marketing and to learn to do what I did as a marketing consultant and direct response copywriter, and that she was eager to come and work for me for free—no pay whatsoever—doing anything for a year if I would let her observe and glean whatever she could from being around me and my operation. Her letter was an outstanding sales presentation, modeled after the techniques and examples I had presented in my speech and in my books and courses sold at that speech. How could you not give this person at least the courtesy of an interview?

Even though I had not been thinking about hiring anybody to do anything, her letter jump-started my interest in having someone around who could function as a personal assistant, researcher, rough draft writer, and "Jane-of-all-tasks."

When I talked with her on the phone, she convinced me that she was serious, sincere, and capable. She got the opportunity she wanted, and she wound up working only for a month without my instituting a low but escalating compensation plan. She was a sponge. She soaked up every ounce of information she could get. Asked a zillion questions. Sat in on my meetings and phone calls. Worked very hard and worked long hours. After about a year, she went on her own and began doing very well right out of the gate. In fact, from her very first consulting arrangement, she was earning between $5,000 and $10,000 a month!

Hopefully, you can see there is a formula here. I'll belabor the obvious. If I were starting out today, knowing what I know now, but with little educational and experiential assets to present, I would target 10 super-successful entrepreneurs or CEOs of small to medium-sized, growing companies in the industry I passionately wanted to work in. I would prepare individual, lengthy letters to each of them, selling myself, and offering to work for free. I'd FedEx those letters to my targets. Then, if I didn't hear from them in short order, I'd start pursuing them with phone calls, faxes, mail, ideas, anything I could think of, in order to secure interviews. And I will bet you the biggest steak in Texas that within 30 days I'd be working for one of these 10 leaders. I'll bet you another steak that I wouldn't be working for free very long.

I had the pleasure of doing some consulting work for and getting to know comedienne and entrepreneur Joan Rivers. One of the things I most admired about Joan was her repeated willingness to start at the bottom and work her way up to the top. After the suicide-death of her husband and the simultaneous cancellation of her Fox talk show, Joan was a pariah in the entertainment industry. No one wanted anything to do with her. No opportunities were available. Her agent dropped her; her calls to contacts went unreturned. The only open door she could find was an invitation to work as a regular on the non-network, syndicated *New Hollywood Squares* for the pitifully low wage of $500 a week. Most celebrities of her stature would have run from such a thing. Seen it as demeaning. Embarrassing. Career threatening. But Joan went to work. It was the beginning of her climb back to prominence, respect, opportunities, and wealth. Joan says, "Walk through ANY open door." She is right.

A Word About Not Taking No for an Answer

In 1975, I was running my own little ad agency and trying to start a publishing company. I was always alert for opportunities to obtain new clients. I happened across an unusual classified ad in which a "millionaire entrepreneur" sought a "writer" who could "put his thoughts, ideas, success, teaching, and philosophy into words" for ads as well as books and tapes. In his ad, he mentioned famous success educators that I had studied, like Napoleon Hill, W. Clement Stone, and Earl Nightingale. I wanted to meet this guy. And I wanted this opportunity—although not as a job, but as a freelancer.

When I called, I was told the position had been filled a week ago. I still asked to speak to this entrepreneur, but I was brushed off. He was too busy and was not available. But I called every day, sometimes twice a day, for two solid weeks. Finally, he invited me in. We subsequently did millions of dollars of business together; he was, in many respects, my best mentor, and without that relationship it is very doubtful that I would be doing what I'm doing today. What would have happened if I had accepted that first brush-off?

Zig Ziglar tells the story of the saleswoman who couldn't hear "No" if it was shouted in her ear but could hear a "Yes" whispered 50 feet away. If you want to fight through the crowd and gain entry to the career field you want, in the company you want, starting out with the attention of top leaders in that company, you need to be deaf to the "no."

I wonder how many job applicants call back 50 times? Or send a new letter every month for 12 months, discussing different reasons why they want to get started in that particular company? I wonder how many applicants are so determined to break into a particular firm that they will continue to try to sell themselves week after week, month after month, for a year or more?

You'll Instantly Have ZERO Competition

The herd of job applicants is plodding through the personnel office, dealing with the human resources folks. You will be the only one talking to the president. The herd of job applicants is "leaving resumes on file." You will be the only one delivering powerful, persuasive sales letters to the top decision maker. The herd never keeps coming back, communicating repeatedly with those who might hire them. You will be the only one not taking no for an answer. Nobody in the herd would dream of working for free for a year. You will have no competition.

This same principle applies to a lot of things other than getting a job. Certainly, to getting a desired client or account or customer. To getting a book published. To solving a problem. Not hearing "no," doing what others won't do, showing up differently, demonstrating tenacity have near universal application. In many such cases, you will be breaking the rules of how that situation is supposed to be handled and how you are supposed to behave. But "supposed to" is for other people—not me, not you.

CONTRARIAN SUCCESS STRATEGY

Neither your college diploma nor your resume has even a penny of value, in and of itself. To get going, you must begin. To get ahead, you must begin. You must get a foot in the door and a hand on some rung on the ladder somehow, somewhere, the sooner the better. A key to success is doing even the lowliest, least desirable job better and with greater zeal than anyone has ever seen anybody tackle that job. Learn to stand out from the crowd in every positive way possible, but most of all, in your willingness to roll up your sleeves and do the dirty work. However, another key to success is leaping, NOT ladder-climbing. You must be alert for such opportunities, recognized or created.

About the Author

D AN S. KENNEDY is a made-from-scratch multimillionaire
serial entrepreneur, having started, bought, built, and sold companies; an active investor including in startups, such as a now
category-leading software firm; and a strategic advisor, consultant, and
business coach to entrepreneurs. He is the author of over 30 business
books and editor of several business and financial newsletters. He has a
40-year track record of guiding entrepreneurs to seven-figure incomes
and personal wealth. As a speaker, he had nine years' tenure on the
number-one seminar tour, appearing with four former U.S. Presidents
including Ronald Reagan, leading celebrity entrepreneurs, and notable business speakers like Zig Ziglar, Jim Rohn, Brian Tracy, and Tom
Hopkins. His own events for entrepreneurs have featured celebrity

entrepreneurs like Gene Simmons, Kathy Ireland, and Joan Rivers. Dan's speaking career includes over 3,000 compensated presentations from three hours to three days in duration, in the U.S. and abroad.

Other Books in the NO B.S. Series by Author

The Best of No B.S. (2022)

No B.S. Guide to Direct Response Social Media Marketing with Kim Walsh Phillips, Second Edition (2020)

No B.S. Marketing to the Affluent, Third Edition (2019)

No B.S. Direct Marketing, Third Edition (2018)

No B.S. Time Management for Entrepreneurs, Third Edition (2017)

No B.S. Guide to Powerful Presentations with Dustin Mathews (2017)

No B.S. Guide to Maximum Referrals and Customer Retention with Shaun Buck (2016)

No B.S. Ruthless Management of People and Profits, Second Edition (2014)

No B.S. Guide to Brand-Building by Direct Response (2014)

No B.S. Trust Based Marketing with Matt Zagula (2012)

No B.S. Grassroots Marketing with Jeff Slutsky (2012)

No B.S. Guide to Marketing to Leading Edge Boomers & Seniors with Chip Kessler (2012)

No B.S. Price Strategy with Jason Marrs (2011)

No B.S. Business Success in the New Economy (2010)

No B.S. Sales Success in the New Economy (2010)

No B.S. Wealth Attraction in the New Economy (2010)

Forthcoming NO B.S. Books

No B.S. Direct Marketing, 4th Edition

No B.S. Time Management for Entrepreneurs, 4th Edition

No B.S. Guide to Successful Marketing Automation

No B.S. Guide to Growing a Business to Sell for Top Dollar

Other Books of Note by the Author

Almost Alchemy: Make Any Business of Any Size Produce More with Fewer and Less (Forbes Books, 2019)

My Unfinished Business: Autobiographical Essays (Advantage, 2009)

The New Psycho-Cybernetics with Dr. Maxwell Maltz (Prentice-Hall Press, 2002)

AUDIO BOOKS are available at Audible.com.

Index